Hope Rises from a Shattered Innocence

Lorraine Taylor

ISBN 978-1-63814-632-2 (Paperback)
ISBN 978-1-63814-633-9 (Digital)

This book is designed to provide information and motivation to our readers. It is sold with the understanding that the author is not engaged to render any type of psychological, legal, or any other kind of professional counseling. The content of each section is the sole expression and opinion of its author, and not necessarily that of the publisher. The suggestions and strategies contained herein may not be suitable for your situation. You should seek the services of a competent professional before beginning any improvement program or if you are currently in therapy.

Covenant Books, Inc.
11661 Hwy 707
Murrells Inlet, SC 29576
www.covenantbooks.com

CONTENTS

Foreword: The Spiritual Journey of Healing from the Bottom of Hell Dr. Paul T. P. Wong, Ph.D., C.Psych

It was an unusually warm Sunday afternoon. As I savored the sunshine and reflected on Lorraine Taylor's book *Hope Rises from A Shattered Innocence*, Francis Crosby's timeless hymn *Keep me near the cross* kept on playing in my head:

> Jesus, keep me near the cross,
> There a precious fountain—
> Free to all, a healing stream—
> Flows from Calv'ry's mountain.
> In the cross, in the cross,
> Be my glory ever;
> Till my raptured soul shall find
> Rest beyond the river.

The lyrics and the music brought tears to my eyes. There is still a well of tears deep in my heart—tears of gratitude to God and tears of sufferings ready to overflow whenever I hear a hymn about God's saving grace or a testimony of another broken human being made whole by God.

The last time I was moved to tears was when I read Laura Hillenbrand's (2014) bestselling book *Unbroken: A World War II Story of Survival, Resilience, and Redemption*. It is a biopic of Louis (Lourie) Zamperini's struggle for survival after he experienced a plane crash and was interned at a brutal POW camp, and his recovery from PTSD and alcohol addiction. Later, when I reviewed the movie adaptation of Hillenbrand's book, *Unbroken* directed by Angelina Jolie, I wrote about faith as the key contributor to Lourie's resilience (Wong 2015):

"Brought up in the Catholic faith, not exactly a practicing Catholic, his faith still sustained him in his darkest hours. His flashback of the homily of the Catholic priest 'Accept the darkness, live through the night, and love thine enemies' was a source of strength and support.

While adrift on the ocean, he said to his two fellow crewmen, 'Pray at night. Pray in the morning. That's how you survive.' Under the blazing sun, tossed around in a raging sea, dying of thirst, and attacked by killing sharks, he dedicated his whole life to serving God, if he saved them. Years later, after liberation, he indeed fulfilled his vow."

Unbroken is relevant to Lorraine Taylor's book because at the end, what saved Lourie Zamperini from the horrors of mental torture and addiction was his faith in the transforming grace of Christ, the one who willingly died on a cross for our redemption.

It is unfortunate that in our sophisticated, scientific community, such beliefs are routinely dismissed as supernatural, irrational, and unscientific without scientific research on the role of faith in God's grace in overcoming addiction and mental illness. There is only limited research on the benefit of perceived forgiveness from God on forgiving others (Krause and Ellison 2003) and on self-forgiveness (Hall and Fincham 2005; McConnell and Dixon 2012).

What really struck me was Lorraine's remarkable transformation in turning her childhood abuse and weaknesses into her strength as a writer and counsellor. Her book was not only written beautifully, but also full of spiritual wisdom and practical help, such as: "Taking time each day to engage in certain practices that develop healthy habits can reduce bothersome symptoms. Regular training with consistency can help decrease anxiety, frustration, depression while fostering emotional, physical, and spiritual well-being."

I often ask myself: How would a child's brain react to the unimaginable horrors perpetuated by people they love and trust, such as parents, grandparents, or priests? How can they cope? Where can they find safety in a dangerous world?

In such traumatic situations, it is probably normal for an innocent and immature brain to shut down, black out, or create an imaginary friend to make the world more tolerable.

I also wonder: What will happen to severely abused children when they grow up? Will they become sadistic criminals because their hearts are full of anger and hatred, bent on revenge against a cruel world which has robbed them of their innocence and hope? Alternatively, will they become depressed, suicidal, or psychotic, because they feel that they are not wanted in this world and they desperately want to hide and become invisible?

I wonder how many people labelled as mentally ill are actually sane and their "crazy" behaviors are actually perfectly rational adjustment to an insane world. As suggested by R. D.

Laing, "Insanity [is] a perfectly rational adjustment to an insane world."

Fortunately, Lorraine's memoir gives me hope that God's love is greater than the worst case of childhood abuse and God's grace is sufficient to transform any broken life.

Although adverse childhood experience (ACE) has received a lot of attention from researchers (Larkin et al. 2012; Zarse et al. 2019) and mental health professionals (Larkin et al. 2014; Lorenc et al. 2020). The most commonly used intervention is based on CBT. However, after reading over Lorraine's spiritual journey of healing, I am even more convinced that CBT would not be able to produce the kind of personal transformation Lorraine has achieved. Here is the extensiveness of the devastating outcome of her ACE:

"I suffered abusive treatment my entire childhood and spent decades as an adult living in the aftermath of this 'hell.'

Witnessing the harmful actions against my mom and siblings' and as a recipient of violence, I was severely affected by Trauma that caused out-of-control behaviors, numerous mental health symptoms, and internal turmoil.

Childhood trauma adversely impacted every single area of my life as an adult. These violent actions resulted in unhealthy thought patterns, distorted beliefs, and hindered consistency.

How I came to view God, a self, others, and the world became sorely warped. I perceived myself through the eyes of the perpetrator."

Here is her description of the futility of traditional psychotherapy:

"Instead of finding myself improving, after years of therapy, I found myself sinking deeper and deeper into this *twisted tornado* of *agonizing torturous living*.

I was eventually diagnosed as mentally ill, with chronic anxiety, paralyzing panic attacks, depressive episodes, obsessive ruminations, and endured years of persistent insomnia.

I experienced intrusive nightmares, flashbacks, diagnosed with CTSD. Eventually, an astute psychiatrist diagnosed me with DID (Dissociative Identity Disorder)—formerly known as MPD—(Multiple Personality Disorder).

Wow, did I feel like a nut with a basket full of mental maladies—all affecting me negatively and significantly impeding the ordinary course of developing as a healthy adult!

Being diagnosed with multiple psychiatric disorders further distorted my skewed concept of who I was. Mental illness intensified the feeling; I was a failure and an abnormally flawed human being. In this prison of Trauma, my life went from bad to worse."

From the perspective of a clinical psychologist, the prognosis of her eventual discovery does not look very promising. I have seen similar cases where victims of abuse spend the rest of their miserable and unproductive lives on medication.

There is limited research on how religious/spiritual coping can have a moderating effect on childhood abuse (Walker et al. 2009) and religious beliefs may play a useful role in childhood trauma recovery within the context of secular psychotherapy (Ross 2016).

But Lorraine needed something much deeper and powerful to transform her life. Here is how she described it:

> "I recognized the missing piece was for me to put to death who Trauma had made me become. In my desperation and helplessness, I discovered the depth of my most essential and necessary need.
>
> I came to recognize the missing pieces and my highest need was to release and let go of this unstable, insecure, beaten down, desperately shattered woman to hide my very life in the safety essence of my Lord's love.
>
> All this time, my Lord waited and wanted to shepherd me, just as he wants to shepherd you. He wants to shepherd us as a community of the people of God in his created vision of a new world, where we relate from his love as our very breath. On that day, I surrendered my madness and the insanity I felt trapped in.
>
> Suddenly in that instant, it was as if a hundred thousand weighted shackles broke, and my blanket of depression lifted. It felt as if an oppressive heavy chain was suddenly cut loose and left my body. The loosing and releasing of this blackness evidenced the spontaneous receiving of his love into the entirety of my being.
>
> I could feel the drawing power of the Lord's love telling me he wanted intimacy, and with me, the woman who felt ashamed and guilty. God let me know he desired communion with me, this woman who felt like a nobody.
>
> I surrendered my anguish, tormented mind, and lost hope to the Lord. I repented of my sins— *idolizing other sources to help me*—in an absolute abandon of who I had become to this stunning and wondrous love."

Her phenomenological experience of conversion is very similar to my own Christian conversion (see more on www.drpaulwong.com) in its immediacy, vividness, and validity. Yes, this was something real happening in our lives, and this transformation was not just some subjective feeling but a fundamental change in our core values, life attitudes, and life goals. It was a transition from death to a shameful self to a new birth in Christ. It represents a re-orientation away from the self and the world to living for God and others; a process similar to self-transcendence (Wong 2016). This new birth marks the beginning of learning how to live a Christ-centered life. Lorraine hastened to add: "In our journey's ebb and flow, we must learn how to navigate challenging obstacles, barriers, road-blocks, and trenches. We must learn to cope with these and the challenging events that happen to us: Trauma, abuses, losses, injuries, mental illness, sickness, death of loved ones, etc."

Throughout this book, Lorraine provided numerous exercises and tools necessary to equip readers to cope with obstacles and develop self-discipline and new habits. She took pains to show that it is an exciting life full of new opportunities and possibilities as we abide in Christ and draw on his inexhaustible resources.

I cannot imagine what kind of courage Lorraine needed to write this memoir and bare her soul. On the day of receiving the fullness of the Lord's love, she stopped hiding, and began the process of healing, growing, and flourishing. She has so much to share with her readers about her spiritual journey.

The take home message from her book is: I am not OK, and you are not OK, but it is OK because we are all vulnerable and imperfect human beings, and our weaknesses could be made perfect by God's grace.

One final thought on healing: Out of the shattering and from brokenness, God's love restored Lorraine to wholeness and oneness. Indeed, effective psychotherapy is about finding a cure for the root cause of human tragedies and suffering; it is about healing our divided self, our divided community, and our alienation from God and nature. Lorraine is attracted to my meaning therapy (Wong 2020a) because it is about the restoration of personal meaning, relationship, and faith through courage, acceptance, and transformation (Wong 2020b).

I highly recommend *Hope Rises from A Shattered Innocence* to all those struggling with childhood trauma and mental health issues. It will not only inform you; it may even awaken you to the hope of finding healing and a new abundant life in Christ.

PREFACE

What is serious to men is often very trivial in the sight of God. What in God might appear to us as "lay" is perhaps what he himself takes most seriously. At any rate, the Lord plays and diverts himself in the garden of his creation. If we could let go of our own obsession with what we think is the meaning of it all, we might be able to hear him call and follow him in his mysterious, cosmic dance.

We do not have to go far to catch echoes of that game and of that dancing. When we are alone on a starlit night; when by chance we see the migrating birds in autumn descending on a grove of junipers to rest and eat; when we see children in a moment when they are really children; when we know love in our own hearts; or when, like the Japanese poet Basho we hear an old frog land in a quiet pond with a solitary splash—at such times the awakening, the turning inside out of all values, the "newness," the emptiness and the purity of vision that make themselves evident, provide a glimpse of the cosmic dance.

For the world and time are the dance of the Lord in emptiness. The silence of the spheres is the music of a wedding feast. The more we persist in misunderstanding the phenomena of life, the more we analyze them out into strange finalities the more we complex purposes of our own, the more we involve ourselves in sadness, absurdity, and despair.

But it does not matter much because no despair of ours can alter the reality of things, or stain the joy of the cosmic dance, which is always there. Indeed, we are in the midst of it, and it is in the midst of us, for it beats in our very blood, whether we want it to or not.

Yet the fact remains that we are invited to forget ourselves on purpose, cast our awful solemnity to the winds, and join in the general dance.

—Thomas Merton, Spiritual Master, *The Essential Writings*

ACKNOWLEDGMENTS

The Lord impressed upon me in March of 2020, soon after COVID hit upstate NY, to begin an online community of believers. I envisioned a gathering to be a safe place where we could grow, learn and come together to hold interactive discussions, ask questions, raise ideas, and share the wonders of God in our lives and in the lives of those we hold dear. What was vital was creating a nurturing environment and atmosphere to foster relationships centered on Abba God's heart. It was equally desired that anyone could ask any question, regardless of how controversial, raise any idea, speak openly about any issue, and feel comfortable with being uncomfortable. And to express that it is okay to not feel okay, and this is part of being a human being.

I sincerely want to thank each individual whose collective voices have deeply touched my life and further centered me in Abba's heart. It has been a wonder to look back over this past year and to see the touch of Father's love upon you and upon us as a beloved community. It has been astounding to view our Lord's grace and mercy in each of our lives and know we are cherished, valued, and accepted. It has been encouraging that I have found each one of you and us as a community to be supportive, authentic persons. It is an astounding reality to see our heavenly Father reveal his deep love, tender mercies, and abounding grace as we share the desires of our thoughts intimately and grow in mutual understanding relationally, providing necessary intercessory prayer.

I name each one in the online community of Faith persons; Barbara, BettyAnn, Deana, Gary, Donna, Michael, Sue, Kim, Marcia, Karen, and Ron. Each one of you has brought meaning to my world as I have seen the revelation of Father's love in your thoughts, words, actions, and deeds. I cannot express in words alone how much each one individually but collectively has inspired hope in the difficulties endured over this past year. In our vulnerable interconnectedness, close bonding, and willingness, we extended this same grace and mercy from our Father to one another as we become image-bearers of a holy God.

To all the other persons I have met through my travels from NY to Florida and to all those I have journeyed with from the state of Colorado, you all have also touched me in ways that have radically altered belief systems and instilled in my heart that God is the miracle of love working in our lives. To each woman in the bible studies at Union Center Christian Church in NY, I am deeply touched by the spirit of Father's love working in and through you, and I marvel that we are intertwined in such bountiful love.

I want to thank my dearest friends, Pastor Fenel and Yolda, for allowing me the privilege to organize, teach and lead Sunday evening services and to be warmly welcomed into your Haitian community of Saints. I want to thank Pastor Herbert Hill JR., his wife Rose, and all the members at Covenant Presbyterian in Kannapolis, NC, for welcoming my husband and me into your fellowship when visiting while providing needed prayer support. We know we have a home and a place in your hearts each time we are in the region, and we are more than touched.

I want to thank Dr. Paul T.P. Wong. Although we never had the opportunity to meet in person, you have influenced and impacted me on many levels. I discovered your instruction and teaching material, along with your faith, to have profoundly changed me in learning, growing, and expanding as a human being. Your dedication to serving and making a difference in others and the world will leave a legacy that will forever change how professionals treat those populations with mental illness. You have made a difference in how therapeutic interventions need to consider the role of faith and spirituality as resilient factors. You have challenged psychological professions to not be so quick to discount an individual's faith as relevant within the counseling framework.

I want to thank each person I have met from the many churches and fellowships around the nation. Each one of you, individually and collectively, has made a difference in my life.

I want to give my sincere thankfulness to my son, Jake, and my daughter, Nichole. You have both brought meaning and value into my world, my life, and our family. I cannot begin to express how grateful I am that with the challenging issues and heartaches we have experienced, we could work through them and redirect our hearts to what is of love, as that is all that matters. Our family is complete, enhanced, and rich, with both of you in my life and in my world. To my son, Lucas, who passed unexpectedly at a young age, you too mean to the world to me and our family. You changed my world too.

Most of all, I want to extend my heart to my husband, Ron. You have stood loyally by my side in all of life's turmoil, and you have helped to make me a better human being showing me a real-life model of what true love looks like. You spoke the truth that challenged, held me near when in tears, and embraced me when I did not know my way. You mean the world to me. Without your consistent, persistent commitment and dedication to our family and me, I would not be the reconciled, restored, and completed woman I am today.

Lorraine Taylor
June 2021

INTRODUCTION

When will this nightmare ever end?
I am living in hell!
Does God even hear me?

These were common thoughts that echoed in my head day in and day out. If you can relate, then you may be dealing with the after-effects of trauma.

I know what it is like to live in this nightmare. I suffered abusive treatment my entire childhood and spent decades as an adult living in the aftermath of this "*hell.*"

Witnessing the harmful actions against my mom and siblings, and as a recipient of violence, I was severely affected by trauma that caused out-of-control behaviors, numerous mental health symptoms, and internal turmoil.

Childhood trauma adversely impacted every single area of my life as an adult. These violent actions resulted in unhealthy thought patterns, distorted beliefs, and hindered consistency.

How I came to view God, a self, others, and the world became sorely warped. I perceived myself through the eyes of the perpetrator. In my mind, I often felt inherently flawed, as if I had a permanent defect, and I often sensed I did not "*fit*" in with others. I carried this "*abnormal*" sense and the nagging feeling I was distinctly different from the entire human race inside me for decades.

Over the years, I had built thick walls where I unconsciously pushed others away from reaching the frightened me, including God and his love.

Enduring the cyclical patterns of trauma, there came a time in my life I felt beyond my ability to cope. I collapsed in utter exhaustion and weariness.

I call this time the "*end*" of stubborn self-reliance and the beginning of learning to abide in the *reign of Christ*.

It was in this place of *surrendered misery* I was finally able to receive the bounty of God's love. His love life became the source of helping me find my way out of this chaotic turmoil and tortured existence.

The material written in this book is written from a Christian worldview and from my experiences in how child abuse caused emotional, physical, mental, and spiritual damage to my person. Although I am a professionally trained master's level rehabilitation counselor and have previously worked in mental health, this book's material uses common ordinary language.

Implementing this book's processes can help anyone. Still, these methods I share are especially beneficial for those who have experienced trauma. This material can benefit those who suffered from childhood, military duty, partner violence, and/or sexual assault.

The exercises and practices shared in these pages have spiritual and human components, where some have scientifically researched affirming results.

As you engage in doing this inner work, you will develop *patience, self-discipline*, and *fortitude*. You will discover an act of courage and resiliency untapped prior. These traits will build strength and equip you with the tools necessary to not give up in the face of wild emotions, questioned doubts, and overwhelming thoughts.

I advise you to read the chapters sequentially and engage in doing this brave work slowly and gradually. When practicing, I suggest you take care to move through the exercises at an even pace before progressing to another.

My hope is that you may be guided in this inside work by God's love and realize you are not alone in moving beyond your trauma.

His love life is the starting place and origin where you and I begin this brave work in leaving the past behind.

I realized my *greatest spiritual need* was to trust God's love. I needed to trust his love was enough to change me. I needed to trust he would do the necessary work to grow me in Christ and lead me into liberty.

My story unfolds in the pages of this book, and the good news is this can be anyone's story, even yours! This story unveils the mercy of a God who offers and welcomes anyone who asks into his grace-filled sanctifying love. I discovered the revealing love of my Lord was the predominant influence who changed me.

> God can do anything, you know—far more
> than you could ever imagine or guess or request in
> your wildest dreams! He does it not by pushing us
> around but by working within us, his Spirit deeply
> and gently within us. (Ephesians 3:20–21 MSG)

I was sentenced by professionals with a lifetime mental illness, *a living "hell."* The diagnosis of DID left me with no cure, no hope, and no way out of *"hell."* I had felt *beyond despairing*.

In my despair, I found that God is faithful. I discovered his love encouraged me to place my mustard seed of trust in him to do the impossible. His love transformed me, a shattered woman.

In the pages of this book, you will read of the unveiling of God's love to me. You will discover how his passion dismantled my faulty belief system. You will read how his love formed Christ in me and carefully moved in my dark hidden places. You will read how his love transformed me in what was deemed a hopeless impossibility into what only God can make into endless possibilities!

Christ longs to shine his ray of hope and grace in your life.

I warmly invite you to read my story.

> When God gets us alone through suffering, heartbreak, temptation,
> disappointment, sickness, or by thwarted friendship—when
> he gets us absolutely alone, and we are totally speechless,
> unable to ask even one question, then he begins to teach us.

> —Oswald Chambers

BRIEF DESCRIPTION
OF EACH CHAPTER

1—Rhythmic Seasons

In the changing seasons of my journey as an adult experiencing trauma from childhood abuse, I did not often awaken feeling a lightened spirit. I did not always appreciate sunshine-filled mornings. This chapter speaks of the various seasons in our lives, and the way forward is often unclear and obscure. Yet, in them, we can tap into the reservoir of courage we were created to hold and trust in a Lord who never fails.

2—My "Hell"

Let me describe how this internal "*hell*" manifested in my everyday world's ordinariness as an adult woman of faith. Even as a Christian, I carried within me a deep-seated sense of rejection and shame. The challenge was to allow God to exchange my self-loathing (that prevented me from receiving love from other people, including God and my husband) with Christ-love. The loving of myself was essential to view God as love, and it would be his love that would be the power needed to change from the inside-out.

3—Truth Is a Person

When we can accept and receive the love God desires to pour into us, we will come into his revelation of what is real. As a person, the reality of Jesus is whose passion pursues you and me and us as a community. This chapter inspires hope that we can rebuild a life according to Christ who is truth, hope, and love.

4—Foundations

Each one of us are products formed from influences stemming from our early childhood environment and family of origin. As a child, we did not choose who would raise us or the type of family we would be born into when abusive actions committed to us became messages received into our core psyche.

This chapter guides learning to move beyond trauma's adverse effects and reorient a life based on the foundation of Christ's love.

5—Fields of Safety

This chapter is significant because it is about safety and places of known caring and trusting. If you reflect on your childhood, there may have been a person, a home, or people who you remember as caring, kind, and compassionate. In this remembering, you will touch upon the critical essential component we need to move beyond trauma—safety.

This chapter takes you back to a time of innocence in my childhood, where I felt and sensed safety, warmth, and love. Suppose you and I can recall such a time. In that case, we can reconnect to those same senses now. These vital connections are necessary for any healing to occur.

6—Misplaced Identity

The biblical view of life is we live in a broken world where bad things can happen even to godly people. Such things occur as accidents, injuries, loss, failure, abuse, trauma, and death.

In the flux of life and when experiencing suffering and painful events, we can still hope in Jesus Christ. We can still believe and trust he is with us in the bad times, just as he is in the good times. This chapter affirms God's love is the only power that can heal us in our emotional, psychological, physical, and spiritual hurt.

7—Forward Momentum

In reality, when needing to change, alter, or modify habits, attitudes, careers, or relationships, one must first be aware of a need to change. Then one must be able to acknowledge what needs to change. Then one must be truthfully honest with themselves. I could not make any changes in my often-destructive behaviors and maladaptive coping mechanisms until I could fully recognize how these behaviors caused negative issues in my marriage, parenting, and other relationships.

In selecting the courageous steps necessary to move forward, I recognized I had to take a different course of action to obtain different results. I placed my little faith and that tiny seed of hope in the possibility of what could happen when trusting God. I chose to follow the potential of where he could take me.

The wealthiest discovery is finding his love is more than able to transform any individual from the messes of life into his beautiful, created, and cherished ones! This chapter guides one to follow the potential of Christ in them by trusting his love.

8—Necessary Processes

Why are processes critical? They are important because they describe how things are done and prioritize steps to take and apply one's mind and body with focused intentionality. Not only are these processes and steps vital, but having a proper attitude in going through these measures is essential. Suppose we can learn how to process life challenges mechanically, integrating the good and bad events and incorporating both light and dark emotions. In that case, we will discover the Lord's grace is enough to enable the transformation needed and wanted.

9—Unlocking Your Self-Imposed Prison

You and I, as believers, are not to depend on human ingenuity (self-made plans and looking to other sources) as guides in the transformation God can perform.

This chapter guides you on the steps needed to reorient and reconstruct your mind, heart, and attitude according to God's holy order and design.

10—A God-Directed Strategy

The misuse of love and wrongly applied power of abuse entangled me in disbelief that God loved me. It was only in trusting and receiving his love, the lies and false beliefs were unveiled. I willingly received God's invitation and trusted his affirming spirit of love, listening to his voice as the agent to lead me out of chaos.

Learning to identify his voice among the chatter in my head and place the small grain of trust in his love was my starting point. His love became the origin and place that restored, renewed and reignited a lost faith. In his love, I found my way out of distorted and skewed truths as he laid the foundation of my true identity only discovered in the life of Christ. My life required reframing according to God's holy order and design.

This chapter guides through the process of allowing his love to dismantle who trauma caused me to become and reorient me from the inside-out—according to his love.

11—Cultural Assimilation

Children automatically, by nature, imitate the ideas and opinions of the culture and environment around them. As a child harmed through years of abusive treatment, I had traits that manifested in distorted thought patterns as an adult driving my often out-of-control behaviors. This chapter affirms that we can overcome unhealthy habits in choosing to think differently and refocusing our attention on Christ's life who fosters spirituality that strengthens and empowers.

12—Habits

To build, develop, and maintain the sorts of transformation possible, I had to do the mechanical part submitting to Christ's love who became the inner source in developing healthier habits. Habits take a long time to grow and take root, and so changing unhealthy habits to create affirming ones may take quite a long time too. There is no rush, no hurry, and no place to arrive. This chapter focuses on the process and steps needed to start and maintain a new habit.

13—An Attitude of Gratitude

How does one obtain an Attitude of Gratitude?

Gratitude is a trait that needs to be cultivated and nurtured. It is rarely mentioned or talked about in Christian circles. Yet, it is a vital component of developing patterns according to Jesus's life. This chapter guides you on how to cultivate and maintain an attitude of gratitude. It begins with being thankful for the little things in life.

14—Mindfulness

Developing a mindfulness practice guides us in not carrying our past in our now and not projecting into a future not available.

Mindfulness is becoming more aware of thoughts, feelings, and sensations in an objective manner where we do not label them as good/bad. When we can learn to distance ourselves and become an observer of our internal realm, we learn to be less judgmental and more allowing of both light/dark emotions. As a believer, inviting God as an active participant with our practices, the Holy Spirit guides us in the transformative processes that lead to lasting changes. Welcoming the truth of our present situation, acknowledging, accepting, and allowing all of who we are, including negatively charged emotions, empowers us to live in the now, taking opportunity to be present in each moment. Scientific research has proven that fifteen minutes of regularly practicing mindfulness a day can change brain patterns where new ones are developed. Growing in our understanding of this practice can greatly impact our bodies' natural ability to heal from past trauma so we can leave our past behind.

Epilogue

In conclusion, this faith is all about being in Christ and not doing. When we press into the unseen yet tangible presence of Christ, he becomes our source in transforming the impossibilities into all possibilities. A life hidden in Christ is a life modeling the love of the Father.

Practices

Taking time each day to engage in certain practices that develop healthy habits can reduce bothersome symptoms. Regular training with consistency can help decrease anxiety, frustration, depression while fostering emotional, physical, and spiritual well-being.

1

RHYTHMIC SEASONS

Hope is willing to leave unanswered questions unanswered
and unknown futures unknown. Hope makes you see God's
guiding hand not only in the gentle and pleasant moments
but also in the shadows of disappointment and darkness.

—Henri Nouwen

One of the first things I do when I wake up in warmer months
is to open my eyes and thank God for another day. I then throw off
the sheets, get out of bed, and go downstairs.

I remember one particular day as I opened our front door and
walked onto our enclosed front porch, sliding the windows wide
open. Standing still, I breathed in a long slow breath of spring air. I
quickly felt the crisp wind brush my face. I heard the sound of chirping birds sitting behind leaves on the branches of the stalwart oaks
that stood guard across the street.

The glistening sun caught my view, and my vision lighted upon
the flittering and fluttering of green leaves dancing in the early hours
of the sky's rays.

Returning inside, I strolled to the kitchen, thankful for auto
settings, grabbed a fresh cup of steaming coffee, and carried it back
to our porch. I nestled contentedly in my seat near the now open

window. I settled restfully and sipped a long deliberate slow drink, savoring the aroma and rich taste of dark roasted coffee.

Mornings such as these, gazing at the graceful swaying of green leaves on branches, listening attentively to the joyous harmony of God's creation are incredibly endearing to me. In those early hours, my thoughts usually turn inward to reflect and consider God.

Sinking into quietness, where the world was still, noise minimal, and most people sound asleep, my stance is one of surrendering to this internal sound of silence.

There are times it is dark when I awaken. Those days before dawn, sitting in hushed solitude, waiting for the first streams of color to appear in the sky, there is contemplative presence.

It is here I touch upon the holy and the divine. It is in these hidden places where my Lord unfolds his tendrils of love. It is in these daybreak moments I sense God longingly waiting to meet me. In these spaces inside, I feel him drawing me near, and I longingly touch his heart in sweet communion.

Recalling those precious times, I thought of how the rhythm of my life churned and fluctuated similarly to the earth's seasonal and cyclical changes. Here in the northeastern US, Earth's seasons wax and wane changing between spring, summer, autumn, and winter. My rhythm beats within this cyclical pattern of changing these seasons as I am continually moving inward in rediscovering God, life, and meaning on a continuum with the earth's recurrent trends.

I longingly anticipate spring after an eternal winter. I look for those first green buds to push their way through thawed soil. My soul beats in an uplifted joy as I walk around my yard, surveying these tiny bursts of new life, soft green, velvety, rising after an interminably frigid winter. Spring lifts my spirit to soar in the unseen realm, meeting the holy.

After the short spring, the lands flourish in shades of green glorious flowers, hotter temperatures, and sunnier skies. Our area offers opportunities to participate in festivals, hiking, water activities, picnics. After the spring, summer is upon us.

Summer eventually wanes into autumn, my favorite time of year, where cooler temperatures array the trees in God's radiant beauty.

Then as the seasons fade into fall, rust orange-burnt leaves cover the ground turning to a decimated dryness. As the winter arrives, the earth becomes layered in a crusted frozenness.

The seasons continue to change in this region where my husband and I have made our home. As humans, we change with the seasons too as we grow and mature in the moments, days, months, and years in our lives' unforeseen circumstances and events. Our journey's changing seasons take us from birth into childhood, young adulthood, our adult years, and finally, our seasoned aged years.

In the season of my early childhood, like you, I had no choice in what type of adults would raise me or what sort of home environment would surround me. Each one of us is born innocent, and we arrive in this world with nothing. Each one of us requires total care and help as newborn babies. We are in utter dependence relying on adults to provide everything we need to survive. Our caregivers change us when we soil our diapers. They bathe, clothe, and feed us in providing for these elementary needs.

In the changing seasons of my life as an adult experiencing trauma from childhood abuse, I did not often awaken feeling a lightened spirit nor could I always appreciate sunshine-filled mornings. My walk in and through this path pressed me beyond my ability to cope and stretched me in ways I felt beyond human capacity to bear the weight.

> Your love, LORD, reaches to the heavens, your faithfulness to the skies. Your righteousness is like the highest mountains, your justice like the great deep. You, Lord, preserve both people and animals. How priceless is your unfailing love, O God! People take refuge in the shadow of your wings. (Psalm 36:5–7 NIV)

The trauma happened to me

In writing of my own experiences with childhood abuse, trauma is what happened to me. *Trauma* is a broad term that covers a wide-ranging spectrum of disorders and conditions. Being traumatized negatively impacts a person and results in numerous emotional/bodily/psychological/spiritual reactions and responses. These have occurred due to the inhumane actions occurring repetitively in a long string of events violating our person done to us as a child.

Trauma does not occur from ordinary, expected, or regular events. Trauma that results from childhood abuse occurs because of persistent, deceptive, and endemic violence acted against us as a child. Its consequences manifest in numerous ways and affect us as an adult, systemically in our bodies, souls, and spirits.

A child needs nurturing to bond, to thrive, and to develop healthy relationships. For a child to grow into a healthy adult, they need caressing, tenderness, and gentle assurance. When a child lacks what nurturing requires, they lack the necessary tools and skills to bond and empathize with others as an adult.

Persistent, consistent, and pervasive inhumane abusive treatments caused a shattering, preventing the healthy formation of my core foundational identity at the most elementary levels. I carried within my body, soul, and spirit the remnants from these abusive actions in my adulthood.

These remnants became systemically *stuck* inside my bodily system (limbic system) in the unresolved collection of emotional/psychological/spiritual wounds. Memories that inflicted poisonous toxins skewed and twisted my inner world in all I experienced, heard, tasted, touched, and felt.

One thing is sure, and research has proven this to be so. Our early conditioning and environment have a lot to do with how we develop and become adults.

I did not have a nurturing, loving, caring, compassionate role model from my earthly father. He gave me no chance of obtaining a cohesive sense of self. I lacked modeling healthy relational bonding from my father to myself, his daughter, so trust, safety, and love were not known or learned traits. Often, I felt as though I was an *imposter* due to the lack of an integrated self.

As a child repetitively exposed to chaotic and violent behaviors, it caused harmful effects that rippled through the core of my being.

The remnants of this type of abuse damaged me in profound ways as an adult. Often in my struggle, I felt at a loss as to how to *"fix"* myself, and I felt *abnormally flawed* from every other person, wondering what was *"wrong"* with me.

In suffering such neglect, I could not sustain contentment, satisfaction, nor did I enjoy a sense of stableness as an adult. I suffered persistent insomnia, little joy, and gloomy days rolled one into another. I could not make any sustainable, lasting, permanent changes.

Raised into a family that exhibited abusive behaviors was much like a constant war, one there was no escaping. I felt helpless and horrifically trapped in this *endemic violence*.

Working on how the remnants of abuse manifested in my adult years in recognizing the numerous facets of how, it had violated my life as a woman was one of the most intense, complicated, and gut-wrenching journeys I have ever experienced.

In struggling through the destabilizing emotions of despair, depression, anger, and social anxiety, with God's help, I managed to overcome what I felt was an *interminable "hell."*

Albert Einstein famously stated, "In the middle of every difficulty lies opportunity."

Over time and through a lengthy process, I willingly allowed God's love to reach into my despairing heart. Like the Good Shepherd he is, he caringly took my hand and led me inward to get out of this torturous *nightmare*.

My heavenly Father's love guided me through the maze of this cyclical *madness* known as trauma.

In this journey, I discovered a more *consistent spiritual practice, a restored mind, and an unfathomable, unimaginable gratifying relationship* with God. This is the God I want to know more resonant, and he is the one I trust as love.

To find my way out of this *"hell,"* I tapped into the tremendous reserve of human courage we were created to hold. I confronted the fears, the lies from the past, and silenced the critical voices. Going deeper into my soul's expanse and caverns, I discovered the hidden treasures of human resilience, fortitude, and perseverance. When I faced those fears head-on, I stopped them from emotional energy controlling and motivating living. I came into an integrated wholeness I had searched decades to find by confronting what most frightened me.

Courage is the most important of all the virtues because, without courage, you cannot practice any other virtue consistently.

—Maya Angelou

2

My "Hell"

I waited patiently for the LORD; he turned to me and heard my cry. He lifted me out of the slimy pit, out of the mud and mire; he set my feet on a rock and gave me a firm place to stand. He put a new song in my mouth, a hymn of praise to our God. Many will see and fear the LORD and put their trust in him.

Psalm 40:1–3 (NIV)

Let me describe how this internal "*hell*" manifested in my everyday world's ordinariness as an adult woman of faith. Even as a Christian, I carried within me a deep-seated sense of rejection and shame. I had trouble loving myself and God. This self-loathing prevented me from receiving love from other people, including God and my husband.

I had trouble conceiving that God loved or cared about me. As a child, my dad's religion subjected me to harsh rules, rote memorization, and constant confessing of *sins*. For decades, my mental image of God mirrored the one I had with my physical earthly dad, distant, angry, and one who held a record of my wrongs.

Not only did I carry the stain of *sin* consciousness in my thoughts and heart, but I had a dad that displayed similar characteristics I attributed to God. This dad controlled our household in rigid unrealistic demands and unpredictable yet anticipated bouts of rage.

To me, the way I saw myself was through the eyes of my biological dad. He was anything but loving or nurturing. The foundational traits that formed my core belief systems came from the brutal messages I received from this monster whose motto was "If you teach a child to fear you before they are three years of age, they will obey you for the rest of your life."

The lies I based my life on became internalized from the violent messages I absorbed into my person from the abuser.

The messages I heard and absorbed were:

- I am not good enough.
- I am ugly.
- I am stupid.
- I can do nothing right.
- I am nothing.
- I am nobody.
- I am rejected.
- I will never achieve anything.
- I will never amount to anything.
- I am unwanted.
- I am useless.
- I am unlovable.
- I am worthless.
- I will never be good enough.
- No one will ever love me.

The force of anger and rage that moved physical, verbal, and sexual assaults (molestation by my uncle) against my person could not be understood or comprehended as an innocent child. These messages became transferred into sensory ones, firmly integrated into my system, and overstimulated my body, soul, and spirit.

As an adult, my internal emotional regulator frequently sounded alarms that fired with bouts of intense fear, terror, and guilt. I battled with a *self-defeating mindset, feeling a lack of worth, out-of-control behaviors, and the inability to obtain consistency throughout my life.*

The more I aged, the more I felt like I was *spinning further* down into this *bottomless dark pit* of no return called "*hell*" on earth.

I wrote the following poem over thirty years ago in describing the *depression* that consumed me and pushed me downward, covering my soul in darkened, thickly laden coldness.

Depression

I feel it.
It starts small
gradually increasing.
My stomach churns
from its sour taste.
My chest caves in
from its pressure.
My mind plummets,
spiraling down, down, down.
Down into darkness
where the stench
smells strong.
Darkness envelopes me—
Draining me of all energy—
It was suffocating me.
Then I come to the place
of lifelessness.
I sit.
My mind races to do something,
but there is nothing to do,
but to feel it,
feel its weight,
feel it stealing me.
It is called depression.

As a young married woman working, raising children, attending church, my symptoms became increasingly severe and complicated. I felt as though there was no hope; I found no escape from the increasing psychiatric symptoms plaguing me.

Those abusive treatments that I experienced had a cumulative effect, manifesting in my day-to-day life, negatively impacting my marriage and other areas of my life. I made many attempts in trying to regain my sanity, my identity, and my life.

There came a time in my life where the internal screams that barraged me could not be quenched or quieted. My desperation caused me to seek out mental health counseling. I hoped that taking this courageous step would help me find my way out of my deep depression and *maddening insanity*.

In proceeding forward with this plan, I placed trust in a man I believed to be a professional and an expert who I thought would be the answer to my dilemma.

Instead of finding myself improving after years of therapy, I found myself *sinking deeper* and *deeper* into this *twisted tornado* of *agonizing torturous living*.

I was eventually diagnosed as mentally ill with chronic anxiety, paralyzing panic attacks, depressive episodes, obsessive ruminations, and endured years of persistent insomnia.

I experienced intrusive nightmares, flashbacks, and was diagnosed with CTSD (Cumulative Traumatic Stress Disorder). Eventually, an astute psychiatrist diagnosed me with DID (Dissociative Identity Disorder), formerly known as MPD (Multiple Personality Disorder).

Wow, did I feel like a nut with a basketful of mental maladies all affecting me negatively and significantly impeding the ordinary course of developing as a healthy adult!

Being diagnosed with multiple psychiatric disorders further distorted my skewed concept of who I was. Mental illness intensified the feeling; *I was a failure* and an *abnormally flawed* human being. In this *prison of trauma*, my life went from bad to worse.

The following poem captures the sense of what it was like living with numerous maladies putting me in the category with thousands of others coping with *mental illness*. This poem was written over thirty-five years ago when I tried to describe this sense.

Madness

I cannot explain this strange
phenomenon.
It twists and twirls,
sometimes,
out of reach of
endurance.
It is like a funnel
burning inside,
frying thoughts.
My heart races to the outside,
my skin sweats.
It pierces craziness
which can only
be felt,
only experienced.
If you have never
been in its grip
you could never know
how it feels.
Confusion, anxiety,
panic, all mixed
into one disorder,
madness.

For decades, entrapped in self-consciousness, I tried to hide beneath a veneer of confidence and competence to appear *normal.* The professionals' diagnostic labels became assimilated into my belief system. These distorted beliefs reinforced my sense that I was a human *defect*; I did not fit *anywhere* or with *anyone.*

I incorporated more lies into my person, believing those "professionals" that I had a lifelong terminal sentence with mental illness and no cure available.

This *secret burden* I tried to bury and keep hidden was due to the fear of public humiliation and scrutiny. In my mind, I believed if anyone ever found out that I had a *mental illness*, that I was not the composed, confident woman I made every effort to display, I would be excluded and banished from all relationships. I believed that surely no one would want to be near me or develop a friendship with someone who viewed themselves as "*crazy*," "*nuts*," or worse, "*unstable*."

Perhaps you are experiencing these symptoms right now. Maybe you are looking at life from behind the bars of this same prison, experiencing inner anguish and turmoil, carrying this hidden secret of *shame*.

I want you to know this is not the real you, the person God created you to become. I want to let you know there is a way beyond this prison and hell.

I took upon myself guilt based on faulty lies. I did not correctly identify it as my perpetrator's, and if you were abused as a child, you might be doing the same thing. Trauma distorts, skews, twists, and shatters our God-created identity.

The only thing that breaks this cycle of shame that silenced my voice and is silencing your voice is to speak and tell the truth. You must tell someone the truth about what happened to you as a child. Telling the truth becomes the *necessary process in moving forward towards healing* on any level.

> The ordinary response to atrocities is to banish them from consciousness. Certain violations of the social compact are too terrible to utter aloud: this is the meaning of the word unspeakable. Atrocities, however, refuse to be buried. Equally as powerful as the desire to deny atrocities is the conviction that denial does not work. Remembering and telling the truth about terrible events are prerequisites both for the restoration of the social order and for the healing of individual victims.
>
> —Judith Lewis Herman, Trauma, and Recovery
> (New York: Basic Books, 1992)

The atrocities of child abuse are horrific. The deeds done to me were carried out behind closed doors and in deeply hidden ways, creating layers of a shame-based foundational identity. Shame to not tell, not talk, and not speak of what happened sentenced me to another prison—*hiding in plain sight behind steel metal bars.*

Shame fostered denial in me as I tried to bury, deny, and dismiss those drastic verbal/physical actions done to me that smothered, destroyed, and stole my childhood.

These cruel *perpetrators'* activities become acted out under a cloak of darkness, which killed, murdered, and imprisoned my voice in a *cold, dark empty tomb.* The collected and stored wounds, scars, and hurts were *silently* carried as a heavy weighted blanket into my adult years—hideous secret atrocities.

After decades of suffering and a lengthy process, it was God's compassionate love who intervened. His Passion grasped hold of me, guiding me to find my way through the *complexity of childhood trauma.*

To find my way out of this cyclical madness, I had to speak the truth, share the pain, accept the hurt, and unveil the shame. I had to boldly take responsibility and own my role in what I could control and learn to let what I could not control go. Making these choices helped me begin my journey on the long road out of this "living hell" to differentiate my part and God's purpose.

Reflective encouragement

On this road, I discovered God's love as my most significant source of help, and I found I could trust him, and I could trust others. You, too, can follow this same path in choosing to place your trust in God, *no matter how frail you feel.* God's love is more powerful than your emotions and circumstances. The road to freedom lies in choosing to trust him over the past. The path to liberty is to trust God in the trauma to bring about his good and perfect will, *regardless of the outcome.*

Trusting God, letting go of results, centering your mind and soul in his love is the way forward and the way out of living in "hell."

Ask today for God to help you, and when you do, trust he has heard you. Trust and believe he promises to be with you in this challenge. His life is the potential of the possibilities of the love of Christ working in and through you.

Grace is the overflowing favor of God, and you can always count on it being available to draw upon as needed.

In all these things, display in your life a drawing on the grace of God, which will show evidence to yourself and to others that you are a miracle of his. Draw on his grace now, not later. The primary word in the spiritual vocabulary is now. Let circumstances take you where they will, but keep drawing on the grace of God in whatever condition you may find yourself. One of the greatest proofs that you are drawing on the grace of God is that you can be totally humiliated before others without displaying even the slightest trace of anything but his grace.

—*Drawing on the Grace of God*, Oswald Chambers

3

TRUTH IS A PERSON

For you are great and do marvelous deeds; you alone are God.
Teach me your way, LORD, that I may rely on your faithfulness; give
me an undivided heart, that I may fear your name. I will praise you,
LORD, my God, with all my heart; I will glorify your name forever.

—Psalm 86:10–12 (NIV)

This hard place in which you perhaps find yourself is the
very place in which God is giving you the opportunity to
look only to him, to spend time in prayer, and to learn long-
suffering, gentleness, meekness—in short, to learn the depths
of the love that Christ himself has poured out on all of us.

—Elisabeth Elliot

Sometimes life is so hard you can only do the next thing. Whatever,
that is just do the next thing. God will meet you there.

—Elisabeth Elliot

In our journey's ebb and flow, we must learn how to navigate
challenging obstacles, barriers, roadblocks, and trenches. We must
learn to cope with these and the challenging events that happen to

us—trauma, abuses, losses, injuries, mental illness, sickness, death of loved ones, etc.

The first word in that sentence is trauma. Trauma is a horrid whirlwind that shattered, annihilated, and destroyed my ability to feel safe, trust, and to accept love, even God's.

The good news is that no trauma, no storm, no trial, no mental illness, and no person can or will ever separate you or me from God's Love.

There is nothing that can ever separate us from God's love. There is nothing from the past, no force, no doubting, no questioning, no mistake, no regret, no mental illness that will ever keep us from the love of God. The harsh adversities we experience now or in the future will never remove God's love.

Scripture encourages us to place our confidence in receiving God's love. It is in the sacred dwelling and fellowship in this place of love where we receive forgiveness, mercy, and:

> No: in all these things, we are completely victorious through the one who loved us. I am persuaded, you see, that neither death nor life, nor angels nor rulers, nor the present, nor the future, nor powers, nor height, nor depth, nor any other creature will be able to separate us from the love of God in King Jesus our Lord. (Romans 8:37–39 KNT)

In the natural, when the darkness of storm clouds dissipates and the sun peaks through the haze and we see the colors of a rainbow, we are reminded of God's love.

As the strange events clatter and clang into our now, we find ourselves in dark places, beyond our capacity to cope; you and I need to remind ourselves God's love will be our firm foundation that grounds.

When you and I face challenging obstacles, we discover in Christ we are granted full provision. We are entirely and sufficiently supplied with all we need. We have everything necessary to live as the kingdom people. When we press in and draw upon the divine power in Christ's love, grace is granted.

> God has bestowed upon us, through his divine power, everything that we need for life and godliness, through these things, his precious and wonderful promises; and the purpose of all this is so that you may run away from the corruption of lust that is in the world, and may become partakers of the divine nature. 2 Peter 1:3 (KNT)

In the light of day, when we respond to his invitation to come, we find a gentle savior who cares for each one, *no exceptions*. We discover a Lord who places within us a yearning for his love that never grows old. Rebuilding a life on truth and love is possible.

> Today is mine. Tomorrow is none of my business. If I peer anxiously into the fog of the future I, will strain my spiritual eyes so that I will not see clearly what is required of me now!

> —Elisabeth Elliot

We can learn to rebuild our lives upon his love as our foundation. Hope becomes tethered and cradled by our Lord's lavish and luxurious forever love. His eternal love enters into all we experience, good and bad, the purity of the Father's heart *embracing* us right where we are, *holding* us ever near, *even in mental illness*.

We discover we can learn to place the smallest seed of trust in his spirit to be a strength that provides *resilience* and *capacity* beyond our own.

Real life originates in Christ, and it is only when you and I yield our weary soul to his fullness we find real life.

The potential of God in me, you, and we as a community of saints are the opportunities and possibilities that lay before us today.

Today is the day of endless prospects. Today is the day where *hope inspires* a journey in becoming transformed. Today is the day *hope* sparks endless possibilities. Today is the beginning of digging deeper into this love, whose life moves us from the old to the new.

The road of God's potential in you and me lies in our love-union *in Christ*. We begin to travel in the new creations as humans the day we receive his love.

The journey he desires to take each one of us on is an incredible, surprising, and astounding lifelong adventurous one. This narrow road of redemption we travel has ups and downs, roller-coaster rides, steep hills, hidden valleys, water-filled gullies, and raging rivers.

Faith is lived in the practical, in the real, and in these cycles and seasons where Jesus promised to begin, perform, and complete his masterful work of art. He is crafting and forming us into radical beings who live from Christ's supplied life, renewed from the inside-out.

He who began a good work—saving you and I and transforming us nearer to likeness in Jesus—is he who will faithfully complete that work, *just as he promised.*

> There has never been the slightest doubt in my mind that the God who started this great work in you would keep at it and bring it to a flourishing finish on the very day Christ Jesus appears. (Philippians 1:6 MSG)

Whenever the grace of God works effectually in a man's inner nature, his nervous system is altered, and the external world takes on a new guise. Why? Because he has a new disposition, he is a 'new creature,' and he will begin to see things differently.

—*Truth & Grace: A Holy Pursuit*, Oswald Chambers

Jesus is faithful to create beauty from the ashes and messes of life

The truth is Jesus, as the master artist, wants to paint beauty from the shattered ashes of our history. Jesus desires to color our world in wonder from the debris and messes. He will perform his highest miracle in revealing his love for each one who asks, *regardless of our past.*

God's authenticity rises in life's darkest seasons and in the adversities, regrets, and shattering of our lives; *he is faithful to do all he promised.*

> For the LORD is good, and his love endures forever; his faithfulness continues through all generations. Psalm 100:5 (NIV)

Light in brokenness

In the cracking, breaking, and shattering is where you, I, and we together as the people of God discover a love that lasts. It is in the *shadows of pain and suffering;* there remains a power that *stretches* and *transforms.*

God's holy being is far-reaching, and his love is amply sufficient to transform you and me from what trauma did to us to our true identity as *Christ-ones.* When we live from Christ as our *no-lack supplier* of love as our starting place and origin of help, we have an infinite reserve assisting us to leave our past behind.

Accepting this invitation in continually receiving his love is our role. Christ will caringly and compassionately grasp hold of you and me, never relinquishing his grip upon us as his beloved, *just as he promised.* The Lord is our Good Shepherd, hovering, leading, carrying, and embracing each one in his constant pursuit.

Jesus loves you and me right where we are and just as we are at this moment. He wants to lead each one of us into the greenest pastures, velvety meadows, and beside quiet pools of water. Jesus desires to place his holy balm of love nourishing and washing the hurt, the wounds, and the scars.

You and I begin this transformative and awakening journey from brokenness. When we accept the tenderness of the Shepherd's outstretched heart and can receive his fondness, affection, and adoration of sweetest love, *his love becomes our home.*

The Lord provides an ardor of love as a shield, going before, guarding behind, and sustaining within by a tremendous grace. His *honey-dripping passion* pours over us, coats our insides, and gently leads us in meadowlands where vast fields of wildflowers unearth an unconventional kingdom.

You and I will never thirst, hunger, or wallow from any spiritual lack. In this kingdom of plenty, boundless treasures and gems will be unveiled. In this new land, the unfolding of the *limitless, infinite, unrestricted, unrestrained,* and *magnified grace* will be revealed in Christ.

Love becomes the birthplace where life transformation spurs the possibilities and potential of new life in Christ. In the grasslands of wide-open opportunities, Christ's life becomes *our way, our truth,* and *our light as individuals and as a community of new covenant believers.*

God-potential births God-possibilities

You do not need to know precisely what is happening, or
exactly where it is all going. What you need is to recognize the
possibilities and challenges offered by the present moment,
and to embrace them with courage, faith and hope.

—Thomas Merton

We have but this day in which to accept this challenge and to begin this journey. This journey leads us inside to discover the unexplored region of who we are in Christ. We cannot possibly comprehend or realize the wealth and mysterious richness to be unveiled. We cannot possibly foresee the wonder, the beauty, and the reality of such love and grace.

There is a vast uncharted space within each of us wherein dwells the Spirit of Christ.

Everything we could ever need for life and
godliness has already been deposited in us by

his divine power... As a result of this, he has given you magnificent promises that are beyond all price, so that through the power of the tremendous promises, you can experience partnership with the divine nature, by which you have escaped the corrupt desires that are of the world. (2 Peter 1:3–4 KNT)

Since these virtues are already planted deep within, and you possess them in abundant supply, they will keep you from being inactive or fruitless in your pursuit of knowing Jesus Christ more intimately. (2 Peter 1:8 KNT)

As an acorn flourishes from its deep roots feeding on earthen fertilizers and grows into a mature tree bearing large branches full of green leaves, so is the potential of the love-seed of faith God has placed in you.

This love-seed of faith is profoundly and tightly rooted in every nook, cranny, and fiber of our being. You and me and we as a community are *in Christ*. Christ grows and transforms us into radical loving people who flourish as his desired ones.

When the acorn is in the ground, one cannot see or tell the beauty, wonder, and strength of this tiny thing. Yet, there is an absolute trust based on experience and past results where we know this acorn will grow into a huge tree. The acorn already contains all that is needed, required, and necessary to mature into a fully flourishing oak tree.

So it is with us. We cannot yet see or realize the splendor, marvel, and intricate depth of God's love revealed in us. We cannot imagine his potential to grow us into our fully formed identity as Christ-ones.

Yet, as the tiny seed within an acorn possess all it needs to grow into a flourishing tree, so do we already have all we need in Christ. His fullness, which is already residing in us, and his love grows us into mature believers. Our need is to realize we have an untapped supply of divine grace whose love grows us into godly image-bearers.

In Christ, grace is always available, always accessible, and is offered to anyone.

We learn to place our trust in his love and goodness based on all the examples of the stories written in the Scriptures of biblical characters who overcame great adversity and struggles.

These stories, other stories, and my account talk about persons of faith who discovered the key to flourishing in this life are found in a Christ who reveals and offers an *empowering strength bearing love-grace*. It is by grace humans become transformed from glory to glory!

> Simon Peter is a servant and apostle of Jesus Christ. I write this to you whose experience with God is as life-changing as ours, all due to our God's straight dealing and the intervention of our God and Savior, Jesus Christ. Grace and peace to you many times over as you deepen in your experience with God and Jesus, our Master. (2 Peter 2:1–2)

We are gifted fullness in Christ. His life gifts the possibilities against all the impossible odds and flourishes God-potential from the shattering and life's messes. It is our Lord who matures us into stalwart oaks, growing us into godly image bearers. The life of Christ is who flourishes in us right where we are planted, *even from suffering*.

> Your potential is the sum of all the possibilities God has for your life.
>
> —Charles Stanley

Establishing a personal, intimate relationship with Jesus Christ is our main priority. We must learn how to tap into this vast unlimited, and fully accessible supplied life in Christ. He is our sole source of sufficiency to help guide us in leaving our past behind. His love forms us into our authentic identity and brings us back home to our true selves.

- Jesus as Lord: "This is how much God loved the world: he gave his Son, his one and only Son. And this is why: so that no one need be destroyed; by believing in him, anyone can have a whole and lasting life" (John 3:16 MSG).

- Jesus as Truth: "But when the Friend comes, the Spirit of the Truth, he will take you by the hand and guide you into all the truth there is" (John 16:13 MSG).

- Jesus as Comfort: "I'm telling you these things while I'm still living with you. The Friend, the Holy Spirit whom the Father will send at my request, will make everything plain to you. He will remind you of all the things I have told you. I'm leaving you well and whole. That's my parting gift to you. Peace. I don't leave you the way you're used to being left—feeling abandoned, bereft. So, don't be upset. Don't be distraught" (John 14:25–27 MSG).

- Jesus as power: "I ask him to strengthen you by his Spirit—not a brute strength but a glorious inner strength—that Christ will live in you as you open the door and invite him in" (Ephesians 3:15 MSG).

- Jesus as source: "Live in me. Make your home in me just as I do in you. In the same way that a branch can't bear grapes by itself but only by being joined to the vine, you can't bear fruit unless you are joined with me. I am the Vine you are the branches. When you're joined with me and I with you, the relation intimate and organic, the harvest is sure to be abundant. Separated, you can't produce a thing. Anyone who separates from me is deadwood, gathered up and thrown on the bonfire. But if you make yourselves at home with me and my words are at home in you, you can be sure that whatever you ask will be listened to and acted upon. This is how my Father shows who he is—when you produce grapes, when you mature as my disciples" (John 15:4–8 MSG).

Reflective encouragement

Our most substantial influence is known when trusting in the Good Shepherd's love. His love offers divine capacity to be the possibility in us. He breathes heavenly potential and endless opportunities for you and me to live by a *spiritually energizing* and *galvanizing grace*.

We all must take risks when standing against fears and emotions that overwhelm. God is the Anointed One who helps you and me accept this challenge to put in the hard work. His love indwells and grants us the ability to put in the effort needed to move beyond the trauma and leave the past behind. The purity of the Father's heart performs the transformation.

I have prayed beforehand and am praying even now for you who are reading this material. I want to affirm that there is no place, no hardship, no crisis, no mental illness, and no trauma where our Lord's loving grace is not enough. Our Lord shepherds us in the good and in the bad. Our Lord gifts a grace that is more than adequate to provide beyond what can even be imagined for you to do this work *(Ephesians 3:20)*. His grace is an unlimited source of supreme, sovereign, and divine influence.

I am praying the following for you even before you picked up this book. And I am praying for you even now that the love of our God will be revealed to you and in you. I pray the evidence of his love envelops your hurt, shame, and pain. I pray you can place the small mustard seed of trust in receiving the genuineness of his care and love.

> My response is to get down on my knees before the Father, this magnificent Father who parcels out all heaven and earth. I ask him to strengthen you by his Spirit—not a brute strength but a glorious inner strength—that Christ will live in you as you open the door and invite him in. And I ask him that with both feet planted firmly on love, you'll be able to take in with all followers of Jesus the extravagant dimen-

sions of Christ's love. Reach out and experience the breadth! Test its length! Plumb the depths! Rise to the heights! Live full lives, full in the fullness of God.

God can do anything, you know—far more than you could ever imagine or guess or request in your wildest dreams! He does it not by pushing us around but by working within us, his Spirit deeply and gently within us. (Ephesians 3:16–21 MSG)

4

FOUNDATIONS

Authenticity is a collection of choices that we have to make every day. It's about the choice to show up and be real. The choice to be honest. The choice to let our true selves be seen.

—Brene Brown, *The Gifts of Imperfection*

Comfort, warmth, caring, compassion was not something I knew with the dad I had. These feelings were only remnants of a long-ago past I knew in my childhood innocence where I could touch upon repeatedly.

And as a child, I was always in need.

I needed acceptance.

I needed to be wanted.

I needed to be loved by my father.

I needed to be nurtured, cuddled, held, and appreciated.

I needed a love that I never received nor was ever shown by my dad.

I spent my entire childhood empty and longing for love. The hollow void in me screamed out to be heard, to be quenched, to be satiated by a yearning for compassion and bonded connectedness.

Perhaps you can identify with this sense.

I never once got what I needed from my dad. I went without his appreciation, his sincerity, his tenderness, and endured a lifetime of sorrow as an adult. My dad went to his deathbed withholding his love from my siblings and myself. I never once saw him show my mother any respect, admiration, or appreciation, and she died long before he did.

Beginnings

We are all conditioned by our early childhood experiences. The type of home environment we were raised in, what kind of neighborhood we lived in, whether we moved around, and what kind of schools we attended shape a large part of who we became as adults.

The type of friends we made, our religion, the culture or heritage we knew, hobbies we become involved in, and the many extracurricular activities help develop and form our inner traits and character. Our personality and who we became were strongly influenced by a combination of many of those factors.

We have learned to value those things that bring meaning and purpose to us were all imprinted into us from the above factors, conditioning us in learned behaviors, responses, and ways of being.

But the most potent influences were the adults who raised us, our home environment, and whether we were raised in a nurturing, caring, safe situation or not.

We were created and designed to be satisfied and fully completed in our heavenly Father's supernatural and transcendent love. When our earthly parent(s) did not incorporate a family model based on love, honor, truth, and compassion, then we will grow up feeling as though we are missing something.

We will hold within our souls a deep dark aching void and a restless emptiness. This empty hole inside us will catapult us into searching for what we never had, and this will be an anxiety-driven relentless longing.

Our desire to have this emptiness of our innermost "*needs*" met with a lost love will dig and eat at our souls. This languid search for a love we never had in our early childhood will consume our waking energies and be continually running in our unconscious, affecting our relationships, pursuits, and goals.

This uncompleted inner void of not having been loved and not having bonded with another will negatively impact us. We will investigate and explore alternatives to fill this sacred space where we miss the bonded connection of love we desired to have in our youth.

I became stuck for many, many years angrily blaming those in my past, especially my dad. I became stuck in a continued cyclical pattern of underlying hostility, irritation, and frustration that often became an infuriating fury.

The self-loathing, deep-seated sense of rejection and endless consuming passions were collective hostile forces of energies I struggled against each day. I was a woman who felt totally and helplessly mentally insane and without hope.

At times, my struggle was *overwhelming, arduous,* and *intense,* much like a chaotic internal *war* in my thoughts and body.

Love that transforms

Each day, I woke in a subliminally unconscious habit of feeding this raging monster within me, its daily food, more anger, more hatred, more bitterness, more resentment. I could never satiate this vicious monster, and as I aged in years, it consumed more and more of my thoughts, attitudes, and behaviors.

Those strong forces of emotions tore at the fabric of my body, soul, and spirit, nagging relentlessly, bit by bit, destroying who God created me to become.

My mind wrestled with so many questions over the years.

Where was God in all this mess?

Why doesn't he rescue, heal, or restore me?

Does God see or hear me drowning?

Did God go AWOL?

Maybe you are asking those same questions now. Perhaps you, too, feel as though God is somewhere distant, far removed from you, and you think he does not care.

Have you ever felt so frustrated, stressed, overwhelmed, or so afraid that you wanted to hide somewhere or bury your head underneath the covers of your bed?

That is precisely how I felt and how I often experienced life under a thickly laden blanket of depressive slumber. It felt like God had left me alone to struggle in this despairing cesspool called life. I experienced emotions that stretched me beyond my capacity to cope. If you can be honest, I bet we can all admit relating to these emotional reactions where we feel as though we are stretched beyond what we can bear.

If someone tells you God does not allow these times, point them to the passage in 2 Corinthians 1:8–11 (MSG). Paul and his team experienced stress and pressure to the point they only saw a death sentence. This sounds very much like the signs and symptoms of a nervous breakdown. Biblical characters are no different from us—mere humans vulnerable to life circumstances enduring impossible situations. We can learn like they did our *need* to rely and depend on a God whose love works in the impossibilities and difficulties we experience. Pressing into grace makes us able to endure all things in him, even trauma.

> We don't want you in the dark, friends, about how hard it was when all this came down on us in Asia province. It was so bad we didn't think we were going to make it. We felt like we'd been sent to death row, that it was all over for us. As it turned out, it was the best thing that could have happened. Instead of trusting in our own strength or wits to get out of it, we were forced to trust God totally—not a bad idea since he's the God who raises the dead! And he did it, rescued us from certain doom. And he'll do it again, rescuing us as many times as we need rescuing. You and your prayers are part of the rescue operation—I don't want you in the dark about that either. I can see your faces even now, lifted in praise for God's deliverance of us, a rescue in which your prayers played such a crucial part. down from the pressures. (2 Corinthians 1:8–11)

Perhaps maybe you have, like Paul and like me, suffered a nervous breakdown(s).

The stresses of life find us inadequate and biblical people were no different. Paul and his team felt beyond human capacity to cope in the unimaginable pressure to the point of certainty that the only end would be death.

Have you ever felt so crushed, feeling as if you were dying psychically, mentally, bodily and spiritually?

I have experienced the brutal agony of such suffering many times.

It is when you and I face situations beyond our capacity to cope there lies hope in a *resilient, faithful grace of an all-sufficient Lord whose love is more than adequate.*

Our Lord waits patiently for us to turn to him. He longs to be our source, our comfort, our life. But he does not force his way into our pain. He respects us. He dignifies us. He honors us. He values us. So he is willing to wait for as long as it takes us to come to him and pour our burdens upon his heart. He waits and yearns for us to sink deeply into his arms where solace is found. Our Lord is more than able to help you and me find peace in Father's heart in the midst of the agony and breakdowns.

Awakening from a long slumber

After cycling in what seemed like an interminable "*hell,*" wanting to change, making changes, but finding no lasting "*thing*" or way that could help me obtain such sustained changes, I came to the end of my self-efforts.

I came to the end of stepping in my ability to figure out how to arrive at what I perceived as being a "*normal*" person. I went through searching in books, looking to people, and sorting through many other things and sources to fill this "*missing*" piece inside—*this deep dark void of emptiness.* Yes, even as a woman of faith, I often felt a restless emptiness.

I can remember that day as if it were yesterday. I lumbered downstairs, totally spent from another evening in never-ending exhaustion from the insomnia plague. I fell, *collapsing* upon the floor, prostrating myself in my foyer with my arms stretched out in *utter helplessness and hopeless despair.*

I cried out in *gut-wrenching gripping* to the God I knew was there, but somehow, he always seemed a bit distant and a bit unreachable. I did not have one ounce of energy left in me nor could I muster any.

Many thoughts swirled through my mind in those seconds, thinking about all that had transpired over those years that had caused devastating consequences, *twisting* my thought patterns, *skewing* my attitudes, and *causing out-of-control* behaviors.

As an adult, I often had trouble recognizing the interconnection between what happened to me as a child and the spasmatic symptoms that daily assaulted me, causing the ensuing insanity in my head.

On that morning, I had finally come to terms with having been abused. I realized the intricate connection between the consequences of its actions and the damage that resulted in me as an adult.

On that day, I *came to the end of myself.* I awakened to what I tried to deny. I stopped hiding. I stopped pretending. I stopped running from my fears and hurts. I stopped running away from God's love.

Vulnerability sounds like truth and feels like courage. Truth and courage aren't always comfortable, but they're never weakness.

—Brene Brown

On that day, I *gave up trying.* On that day, I intimately realized and recognized my spiritual poverty. I recognized my *need for God's love.* I admitted my failure in owning my role and taking accountability. I confessed neglecting God as the source of help. In my heart, I knew his Spirit groaned and agonized with me.

It was God's love who led me in *letting go* and recognizing my real *need.* It was my heavenly Father who ushered me to this state of heart wrenching pain in being b*eyond done. God's love helped me release resistances, the struggling, and the battling.*

Father's holiness drew me to a place where I was able to let go of the paralyzing fears, crippling anxieties, debilitating panic episodes, and the sinking pit of depression.

In this place of surrender misery and shattering, I discovered the beginning of the end of self-independence. I encountered an embracive warmth enveloping me in God's love. The fragrance from Father's love announced forgiveness and emancipated goodness, sweetness, and merciful tenderness.

This place of God's love is discovered in receiving and in *surrendering*. I finally was able to let go of what trauma caused me to become—*a shattered, debilitated, shamed woman*. In laying aside my will in this way, he led me to understand my *"need"* was to dwell in the place of the perfect, pure, chaste, holiness, and faith of my heavenly Father's love.

> Faith is more than an attitude of the mind; faith is the
> complete, passionate, earnest trust of our whole nature
> in the Gospel of God's grace as it is presented in the Life
> and Death and Resurrection of our Lord Jesus Christ.

—Oswald Chambers, *Truth & Grace: A Holy Pursuit*, pg. 74

Resolute love

This releasing and this turning over of all the craziness, all my spent energies, and all the decades of inner turmoil was the *end of a long, dark, cold, hibernating death of my soul.*

I recognized the missing piece was for me to *put to death* what trauma had made me become. In my desperation and helplessness, I discovered the depth of my most essential and necessary *need*.

I came to recognize the missing pieces and my highest need was to release and let go of *this unstable, insecure, beaten down*, desperately *shattered woman* to hide my very life in the safe essence of my Lord's love.

All this time, my Lord waited and wanted to shepherd me, just as he wants to shepherd you. He wants to shepherd us as a community of the people of God in his created vision of a new world, where we relate from his love as our very breath.

On that day, I *surrendered my madness and the insanity* I felt trapped in.

Suddenly, in that instant, it was as if a hundred thousand *weighted shackles broke*, and my blanket of depression lifted. It felt as if an oppressive heavy chain was suddenly cut loose and left my body.

I could feel the drawing power of the Lord's love telling me he wanted *intimacy*, and with me, the woman who felt ashamed and guilty.

God let me know he desired communion with me, this woman who felt like a nobody.

I *surrendered my anguish, tormented mind,* and *lost hope* to the Lord. I repented of my sins—*idolizing other sources to help me*—in an *absolute abandon of who I had become to this stunning and wondrous love.*

With *God's holy love*, I found my way out of this *cyclical swirling insanity*. This journey began learning to receive his love and then bit by bit, *letting go of* the *lies* and the decades of a relentless emotional "*hell*."

Wrapped, enveloped, and immersed in such love allowed me to let go of those emotions. I encountered the most majestic, wonderous spirit and on that day, I entered the reign of *Jesus's unwavering, ravishing, and abounding love.*

Revealing love

> God will never reveal more truth about himself until
> you have obeyed what you know already.
>
> —Oswald Chambers

Although I had known Jesus for decades, encountering the reality of his presence at age nineteen, this new revelation of his unconfined and liberating love in my mid-fifties allowed me to *surrender my struggling.* I saw a greater *need* to stop believing the lies and surrender what trauma had made me become. These new levels of understanding brought me to a fresh perspective in my view of God, self, and the world.

After many years of enduring the *dark, cold, hibernating death of my soul,* the Lord birthed an incredible redeeming sweetness of his Spirit blended in mine. His hand reached into my ongoing cycles of *madness,* rescuing me from that gloomy *"pit,"* the impermeable life sentence of mental illness, and led me into *luscious green fields* displayed in the poetic passage written in *Psalm 23.*

My ability to survive in the face of what professionals told me was an incurable mental illness was a miracle from God. Having a diagnosis of no hope from the medical community and the miraculous intervention of God's love was indeed a *tribute to his mercy* and the revelation of his *redemptive saving grace.*

In receiving *his revelatory love and trusting in this love,* God helped me overcome the past. I allowed the supernaturally influence of his Spirit to perform a radical and miraculous work inside the wounds, hurts, and scars. Over time, I was healed from the adverse effects of what trauma did to me.

In Christ, I recovered from the effects of a lifetime of child abuse and also totally and completely *healed* from one of the most severe and persistent mental health disorders called DID (*Dissociative Identity Disorder; formerly named MPD—Multiple Personality Disorder*).

Encountering and receiving God's empowering love was *powerfully life-altering* and a *radical transformative journey. This was my arrival into a new way of being and discovering a new me, the one I had longed to be.* In Christ, I was finally freed from bondage that lasted a lifetime.

Resounding love

In receiving the fullness of his deep love, my Lord Jesus took my hand. He led me into the greenest pastures and lushest meadows spoken of in Psalm 23 where he *reignited a lost faith* and inspired a *revived hope.* His love led me to live in the land that flowed with the creamy taste of milk and honey.

This new land discovered in God's kingdom was where Father's love freely and unreservedly flourished and abounded as a significant source of change in my life. I encountered a holy order where life and truth became measured according to a union in the Godhead (Father, Son, and Holy Spirit). In this dwelling, I discovered the sacredness of holiest, divine, real love.

This *transformative journey* is a never-ending process and one I am continuing to explore, investigate, and participate in and with. Jesus continues growing me into his fullness. His love continues to unfold the shiniest pearls and brilliant riches of the Father's heart.

On that day and in the surrendering, I crossed over the river from where bondage of abuse enslaved me to a new kingdom. Arriving in this new land, I obtained lasting *freedom* from the deep love of a Lord who *reigns in righteousness* and *grounds by mercy.*

I began that day understanding *my role and my responsibility* to live such a *renewed life*; I would need to appropriate a *profound living grace.*

Whenever we obey, the delight of the supernatural grace of God meets our obedience instantly. Absolute Deity is on our side when we obey so that natural obedience and the grace of God coincide. Obedience means we bank everything on the Atonement, and the supernatural grace of God is a delight.

—Oswald Chambers, *Grace & Truth: A Holy Pursuit*, pg. 83

5

Fields of Safety

The Lord is my shepherd. I always have more than enough. He
offers a resting place for me in his luxurious love. His tracks
take me to an oasis of peace, the quiet brook of bliss. That
is where he restores and revives my life. He opens before me
pathways to God's pleasure and leads me along in his footsteps of
righteousness to bring honor to his name. Lord, even when your
path takes me through the valley of deepest darkness, fear will
never conquer me, for you already have! You remain close to me
and lead me through it all the way. Your authority is my strength
and my peace. The comfort of your love takes away my fear.

—Psalm 23:1–4 (TPT)

Travel with me back to a childhood period where I can recall
such inner calm, safety, and peace. I would like you to walk with me
to a time and place I knew innocence and sensed contented quietness. I remember the places and people in those times as some of the
most meaningful memories I experienced as a young child.

This place was a land filled with what I felt was God's luscious
green grasses, spacious in vast forested woods, and long golden fields.
These lands, located in the rural countryside of Pennsylvania's rolling
hills, filled my heart with satisfying sanctity.

It was in those rustic hills I roamed as a child, walking proven paths of generations past, I felt secure. These lands where my great-grandparents settled filled me with liberating freedom. I could ramble for miles walking in those wooded hills alone. This place fondly referred to as "*The Farm*" was the homestead of my kin, soundly planted in the middle of 160 acres of pristine wilderness—a secluded respite, an oasis where I flourished as a young child.

I had not been to those hills nor had I visited since I was a child. As a young married woman, my heart often longed and yearned to once again stand on the land that belonged to my kin. I anticipated a time to walk with my husband and show him the small house my great-grandparents built and take his hand and walk down the rough stone driveway where Grandma and I picked berries to have with our breakfast.

I would fondly tell my husband about the velvety green fields that were sectioned off by an old stone wall, remnants of the war fought in those hills where my grandpa and I crouched near to view the deer at dusk through his binoculars.

In my mind, I can picture my grandfather meander slowly out to the field past the stone walls, and I was walking beside him, hearing him whisper for me to be still so as not to scare the deer away. We would wait in anticipation of the first sign of the deer's brown color, then my grandpa would peer through his binoculars to get a closer view, passing them to me so I could also look through them.

Such bonding existed near my grandpa who took time to be with me, showing his tender caring. Slowly strolling with him as if he had all the time in the world, out to the second field so I could view the deer just before dusk, settled my heart.

So many times, we walked to those fields together, and each time was like the first; my heart was palpitating excitedly, my eyes alert, my attention fixed, and my gaze straight ahead. Closing my eyes now, I can see those fields, retrieving the distanced memories from those fifty plus years ago. If I slow down, breathe deeply, I can smell the fresh country air, feel the breeze fashioning my hair, and picture the colorful array of wildflowers dancing in their beauty.

Those recollections of all the people I loved and the pictured wilderness have left indelible impressions as fond images, sensations, and hidden pleasures I tucked away in the corners of my mind. In thinking back to that season in my life, I could immediately bring these memories to my present thoughts, enjoying a distinctly different time in my childhood.

It was in that rural county of Pennsylvania I received peace from nature, God, and older ones—grandparents, great-grandma, and my favorite great-uncle.

The house itself was a historic piece of my past. Visiting those scenes, those images, those hills I walked was done as often and as frequently as I could in my mind, I could go there anytime, and all I had to do was remember, consider, reflect. In my troubled adult years, I could be still and breathe in the sensations of a long-ago safety I knew in those wide-open spaces. These memories would join the thin, tattered threads of my present with feelings of long-ago liberty and innocence that I needed to have in my then adult years.

After coming over to America from the Dutch land, inside the house built by my great-grandparents was a sizeable double-barrel woodstove. The stove was used for all our cooking, being fed wood from dawn to twilight.

There were no modern conveniences such as electricity, plumbing, or A/C. Kerosene lamps were strung around the living room, dimly lighting its contents. For the bathroom, we had to walk out the front door, around to the back of the house, and down the hill to the two-seated outhouse guarded by two healthy Shag Bark Hickory trees.

I always wondered why two seats as I never went in there with anyone else, could not imagine two people sitting so close together. Porcelain bedpans were neatly positioned underneath our beds to go to the bathroom at night.

When not sleeping in our family tent, I slept in the double poster bed upstairs, just down the hall from my great-grandmother's room. Her room was sparsely decorated with a twin bed, neatly made, a small bureau where her Bible, rosary beads, and a brush laid.

After snuggling into the comfort of the poster bed at night, I often found myself transfixed by the clarity of the sky as I peered out the window. Zillions of stars dotted the blacker than black blanketed night sky. Glowing as fires, each one, shining little specks of light, glittered and sparkled in my tiny head.

Cozily settling underneath the sheets, having had my day in the wilds, full of sunshine, walking, picking berries, or just sitting on the open front porch, I would snuggle deeper for a restful sleep. Heavenly respite: comfortable, warmed, relaxed, safe.

My great-grandma was a devoted woman of the Catholic faith, walking the six miles on dirt roads to attend the rural church Sundays. I can imagine her with a Bible in hand, a smile on her face, and prayers in her heart, walking those dirt roads to gather with others in that small country church. I am sure she persisted interceding in prayer for me and others day in and day out.

Such was the case where my family traveled that same path to attend the same local church with her when visiting "*The Farm.*" Wherever we vacationed other places, the mandate to participate in the local Catholic church was a stated requirement. Our generation followed generations of old, the good and faithful men and women from centuries past steeped in ancient traditions.

Upon coming downstairs, those mornings, my senses would be ignited with the strong smell of bacon sizzling in the frypan and the scent of fresh-brewed coffee drifting into my nostrils. Images of my great-grandma sitting in her rocker quietly near the sunshine window and watching the other adults prepare breakfast saturates my thoughts even now.

My Uncle Joe would be feeding his mash to the many stray cats that remained nearby, licking their lips, waiting expectantly for this delicious mixture. He regularly cooked, morning and night, leftovers or strange stuff. I had no idea what it was, but I was sure humans would not touch it.

I can remember many of the minute details of what seemed to be a simpler life in those rolling hills of Pennsylvania. Such was my pleasure and joy to spend time there; I would do anything to go to the farm. I would even ride with my great-aunt, her dog, and the windows rolled up almost closed. She barely drove over forty-five miles at the highest speed, and I often felt smothered by the smell of the stifling summer air.

You might want to know back in the 1960s; cars had no A/C. I weathered the suffocating car ride, the pungent overwhelming dog smell, and the musty old vehicle to get a trip to my most favorite freeing space in the entire world, Great-Grandma's "*farm!*"

It was affectionately called "*The Farm*" by all family members because at one time, it used to be a working farm with cows, chickens, vegetables, and all that went along with that. I never knew my great-grandpa as he had died in 1929 from the Spanish flu that whipped through that region, taking many men by its grip of death.

Thriving in those moments, hours, days, and weeks spent on those lands were enough to recall the many pleasures I spent in a more comfortable life. These were the memories I especially visited from those early childhood years and repetitively so in tumultuous times. The depth of my pained struggle and battling in my adulthood was intense, ongoing, and seemingly had no end or relief in sight.

I cherished the stories of generations past my grandma relayed to me. She would tell me of her day rising before dawn when it was still dark to help with chores before making the six-mile trek to the one-room schoolhouse she attended as a child.

I am not sure what passed for snow leggings then, but she said in winter, by the time she trudged through the high drifts, her pants were sopping wet.

Upon arriving at her one-room school, Grandma would take them off and hang them to dry near the wood stove in the center of the room, taking the entire time she was in school to dry. When the time came for her to return home, she put her leggings back on for her long walk through those same drifts.

Wow, to think my grandma had to walk twelve miles each day to attend school in all kinds of inclement weather and this after getting up early to help her mom with farm chores. Imagine how tired she must have been at the end of the day, and in the winter season, how dark it must have been when she got home.

Those shared times at "*The Farm,*" when things seemed more relaxed, less complicated, and families remained strongly interconnected through the seasons of marriage, children, grandchildren, and great-grandchildren are fond memories. I have neatly tucked them into the folders of the many envelopes of stored favorites in my thoughts, and I open them to view their contents time and time again.

Noiseless sanctity

Reviewing and reliving those years refreshed my spirit, lifted my mind, and relieved worn exhaustion from the stress of living as a traumatized young woman, trying to find my way in my mixed-up dysfunctional psyche.

Remembering, reflecting, pondering would take me back, way back to the innocence of laughter, the timeless joy in playing, the hours of conversing with elders I loved and appreciated.

Senses of memories flooded and became deposited in my thoughts, settled in the core of my being, gave me a hint of a safe solace.

The space inside me I could go to be quiet, to be me, to know peace was of comfort during the cumbersome complicated mental health world I became *stuck* inside due to the many facets of how Trauma manifested itself in my adult life.

Hopefully, we all can think back on our journey and try to remember the unique places. Recalling those distinct caring people who bring warmth rising inside us can help us not forget the sense of safety. We can rewind the tapes in our minds and visualize those memories as sacred spaces that hold images restoring us to known sanctuaries.

I did this meditation exercise quite frequently. I was unaware that was what I was doing, but I naturally sought those same emotions, the same liberty, and the same pleasures I did in the long-ago innocence of my childhood in my adult years.

I longed and yearned to return to those lands, to walk the dusty dirt roads, and to once again ramble in those forested woods. My heart ached to once again walk on those wide-open fields and view the wooded forests where I tasted peace, contentment, and joy. I longed for the bonded nurturing I had sensed in inter-generational relationships and neighboring farmers.

There were decades spent living in the dark depths of my soul where I purposefully conjured up those memories in allowing them to be what centered my thoughts, heart, and body. Reaching into those tucked away images in my mind was like trying to return and find the missing pieces of life in spaces of remembered safeness.

"*The Farm*" was a *special holy* place to me, and I often played the images again and again inside my mind. I often prayed in earnest, longing to know once again the feeling of sanctity and solace I had as a child who thrived in this place where my ancestors farmed. I yearned to somehow transfer those protected images and feelings into my thoughts and heart as an adult.

In a world of noise, confusion and conflict it is
necessary that there be places of silence, inner discipline
and peace. In such places love can blossom.

—Thomas Merton

Reflective pause

Take a moment now to reflect and reach back into your past. Close your eyes and breathe deeply, think, and consider if you have ever sensed or felt a time of peace, joy, or known someone who cared or loved you. Perhaps a grandparent, a relative, neighbor, teacher, leader, or friend in your community. Maybe you can remember a trip, some experience, some "place" that made you feel at home, at rest, and at peace.

Try and capture that sense and hold onto it. Think about smells, images, feelings, sensations, and what comes to your mind. Hold the safeness with you and embrace it as this lends hope, and these sensations can help you remember a bonded connection with love. The remembering of safety and carrying that sense of what it feels like to be held, embraced, and wanted lends hope. There is hope found in our Lord's lavish and luxurious love. It is possible to be restored, renewed, and revived from this love.

The transformation you and I want and need begins in receiving and trusting Father's love. When you and I ask, God has promised to reveal to each one *the height, depth, width*, and *breadth* of his consuming fire of passion and love.

We, of course, have plenty of wisdom to pass on to you once you get your feet on firm spiritual ground, but it's not popular wisdom, the fashionable wisdom of high-priced experts that will be out-of-date in a year or so. God's wisdom is something mysterious that goes deep into the interior of his purposes. You don't find it lying around on the surface. It's not the latest message, but more like the oldest—what God determined as the way to bring out his best in us, long before we ever arrived on the scene. The experts of our day haven't a clue about what this eternal plan is. If they had, they wouldn't have killed the Master of the God-designed life on a cross. That's why we have this Scripture text:

No one's ever seen or heard anything like this, Never so much as imagined anything quite like it—What God has arranged for those who love him. But you've seen and heard it because God by his Spirit has brought it all out into the open before you.

The Spirit, is not content to flit around on the surface, dives into the depths of God, and brings out what God planned all along. Who, ever knows what you're thinking and planning except you yourself? The same with God—except that he not only knows what he's thinking, but he lets us in on it. God offers a full report on the gifts of life and salvation that he is giving us. We don't have to rely on the world's guesses and opinions. We didn't learn this by reading books or going to school; we learned it from God, who taught us person-to-person through Jesus, and we're passing it on to you in the same firsthand, personal way. (1 Corinthians 2:6–13 MSG)

6

MISPLACED IDENTITY

Define yourself radically as one beloved by God. This is the
true self. Every other identity is illusion. God's love for you
and his choice of you constitute your worth. Accept that,
and let it become the most important thing in your life.

—Brennan Manning

It's in Christ that we find out who we are and what we are living
for. Long before we first heard of Christ and got our hopes up, he
had his eye on us, had designs on us for glorious living, part of the
overall purpose he is working out in everything and everyone. It's
in Christ that you, once you heard the truth and believed it (this
Message of your salvation), found yourselves home free—signed,
sealed, and delivered by the Holy Spirit. This signet from God is
the first installment on what's coming, a reminder that we'll get
everything God has planned for us, a praising and glorious life.

—Ephesians 1:11–14 (MSG)

The Bible realistically informs us, even in Christ, we will suffer
pain and experience trials in this world. The biblical view of life is we
live in a broken world where bad things can happen even to godly
people—accidents, injuries, loss, failure, abuse, trauma, death. In all

of these things, we can still hope in Jesus Christ, knowing the truth that he is with us in our pain and sorrow. His love is the power that can place a holy balm of healing in our emotional, psychological, physical, and spiritual hurt.

In the Gospel of John 16:33, Jesus told his disciples, "I've said these things to you so that you can have peace in me You'll have trouble in the world. But cheer up! I have defeated the world" (KNT)!

In this passage, Jesus offers words of hope and truth amid trying circumstances. Although you and I suffer due to people who have chosen evil over good (or poor choices), we can avail ourselves of the invitation Jesus offers to each one in receiving this otherworldly love. God's love is more powerful than the forces we are struggling with due to trauma, and his love is the most precious and treasured gift we can ever receive and discover.

This gift is available to anyone willing to receive, and there is not one exception. All human beings are included in Father's Salvation purposes. His love reconciles, holds, enters, unites, and embraces.

As a Christian, my worldview is that the result of this world's sin and brokenness is the root cause of tragedies and inhumane suffering. Traumatic events can happen to anyone, including Christians. Trauma distorts our perception of God, ourselves, the world, and others. In experiencing developmental trauma, my sense of safety and trust became shattered.

In repetitive exposure to adverse experiences as a child, the cumulative effects negatively impacted psychosocial and cognitive development areas. Instead of having a sense of openness and wonder as a child, rigid and stringent beliefs formed that prevented me from viewing myself as lovable and competent.

Belief

Belief is defined in Webster's dictionary as "something one accepts as true or real; a firmly held opinion or conviction."

What we believe to be true does not necessarily mean it is the truth. Our beliefs are formed from a young age as we receive environmental stimuli into our bodies.

Our home environment has the most substantial influence on us in our early years of development as a child. We automatically and naturally absorbed into our bodies the messages we heard, saw, and felt at a sensory level in our preverbal years.

The beliefs that formed the early foundation of my personality resulted from repetitive exposure to violence. The destructive force and inhumane actions towards me from my dad resulted in constant feelings of anxious fear and impending danger.

Raised in a hostile environment left me little to no opportunity to develop feelings of being loved or feeling a sense of safety in my own home. As I matured in age, the lack of bonding, and connection with my biological dad in those early years left me with a sense of emptiness and loneliness. I could not develop an attachment to basic human needs such as love, trust, or safety.

As an adult, it seemed I spent a lifetime searching to discover what I felt was a *"missing"* ingredient in my life that I could never quite describe. I never felt completely satisfied or fulfilled. I never felt at home in my own body.

The beliefs I incorporated at the core level were extremely dysfunctional ones, which only led me to adopt coping strategies and dysfunctional methods. Maladapting coping skills caused severe problems in my ability to experience close relationships. I had to deal with persistent mental health issues as an adult.

As a traumatized child, the core beliefs resulting from trauma were formed based on violence. I did not choose these beliefs. These core beliefs included the thoughts and assumptions that I held about myself, others, the world around me, and God. Each one of us has core beliefs. These deep-seated beliefs often go unrecognized, and yet they always impact our lives. These beliefs continually run in the background of consciousness as a constant moving stream of thoughts, ideas, and values.

Values

The core values that I held came from these core beliefs. Core values are a set of *principles* that dictate behaviors. These values help you and me to know what is right from wrong; they create an unchanging guide that directs one's moral compass.

Beliefs and Values

As a Caucasian child raised in a dominant Caucasian environment, I inherited a worldview from my family of origin. My early influences with the forced religion by my dad; his rigid mindset and violence instilled false beliefs and values. I was also strongly influenced by the environment around me, such as the tumultuous and opportunistic period in America's history with the Vietnam war, the Cuban missel crisis, civil rights, and the assassination of MLK and JFK.

Other factors that were occurring in that time period that affected me were that women were not viewed or treated as equal human beings in relation to males. This was the case in my home, in the church, in the workplace, and in general throughout American culture.

In my adulthood, I encountered a living, loving Jesus and began my path unlearning the inherited beliefs that God was an angry, vengeful being. I had to relearn what was true according to my encounter and reality experienced when the Lord touched the core of my being with an embraced inclusion, where I knew, without a doubt, this being named God was filled with the purity of a holy divine love. This awakening to his passion left me a changed woman as I knew, without a doubt, the God who pursued me and the God who filled me was a spirit being, who was all forgiving and all loving.

(Note: One's worldview is vital when choosing a professional to help you work through trauma and what happened to you. It is important you select a person similar in belief systems and values to those you hold as true.)

In the Christian worldview, the central core beliefs I held was a belief in a single being and *eternal* personal God. This God is true, living, all-wise, all-powerful, a supreme spirit and sovereign over all forces, darkness, persons, or "thing" created.

This personal God *created* the entire universe, including human beings, and established *moral principles.* These principles were written in the Bible to guide people to treat one another with *value, dignity, respect, and love.*

Christians worship this single God in *prayer, reading, worship, fellowship, and meditating on Scriptures.* Believers carry out their devotion to this God in conversation, thought, and relationships with one another and in community.

A biblical core value is God loves each individual created, regardless of behavior or one's past. As a Christian, I believe God is a reconciling spirit whose purpose is restoring human relationships with divine holy order and redeeming love.

> This is how much God loved the world: he gave his Son, his one and only Son. And this is why: so that no one need be destroyed; by believing in him, anyone can have a whole and lasting life. God didn't go to all the trouble of sending his Son merely to point an accusing finger, telling the world how bad it was. He came to help, to put the world right again. Anyone who trusts in him is acquitted; anyone who refuses to trust him has long since been under the death sentence without knowing it. And why? Because of that person's failure to believe in the one-of-a-kind Son of God when introduced to him. (John 3:16–17 MSG)

How God relates to humans and his character can be discovered by reading biblical stories. God also reveals himself to each one who asks. In our limited view, we often do not understand nor can we fully comprehend his activity in our lives or the whys in the vast amount of suffering in this world. We can barely believe we could be so loved, wanted, or desired.

As a believer, I recognize that he alone knows the purposes and intentions for my suffering, your suffering, and the suffering we encounter in other's lives. I believe God is intimately involved in all aspects of life, including every individual in this world. Still, he never forces the offering of this gift of love on anyone nor does he force anyone to believe in him.

I think only God understands why seemingly "good" persons suffer. It is my opinion, only God knows reasons behind this suffering that are often incomprehensible or unknown to us as humans. There are not always lessons to be learned in the suffering. Suffering is and will always be part of life as a believer.

In professing Christ and then following the way of faith in my trauma, I had problems viewing God as a father figure. When a pastor or another believer mentioned God as our Father, I wanted to run from the church as it made me want to vomit. I had mistakenly identified Father God with the dad I knew who was anything but kind, gentle, compassionate, caring, or loving.

It took a very long time; in fact, it was not my mid-fifties where I was able to fully receive this love and view God as a caring, kind, and good heavenly Father. In accepting and receiving into my being the fullness of this love, I came to view God as love. I slowly began to see myself through the filter of this same love. Then I began to view life and others through this same love lens.

These facts are an essential consideration when speaking of God to realize that when a person has suffered trauma, they might be viewing God as a not-so-good Father.

This book is not a theological one, but I must define my worldview as a Christian in what I believe so you might understand where I am coming from.

The Bible refers to God as a male in its masculine use of language, and Jesus referred to God as Father. The Bible writes of God in the masculine gender as a pronoun, and the masculine has been used for written communication historically.

In my opinion, I believe that God is not in human form but is a spirit. The New Testament confirms this idea in the Gospel of John: "God is sheer being itself—Spirit. Those who worship him must do it out of their very being, their spirits, their true selves, in adoration" (John 4:24 MSG).

In my view, God embodies all facets of humankind, the feminine and the masculine. God is a spirit-being, and as a spirit is genderless. In my view God is the full expression of the diversity, uniqueness, and specialness in all humanity he created.

Allowing Father, Jesus, and Holy Spirit to reveal their union and love is a lifelong journey. I am awed, honored, and privileged to co-participate as a desired and wanted one in this love nature. Each moment, I willingly receive their love and allow expression of this love to be manifested to me, a woman who was shattered but became restored according to their love, and from this love, I am now integrated and whole.

Core foundational beliefs I struggled with: trust, love, and safety

1. Trust: Deeply ingrained into my persona and early developmental growth was; I cannot trust others. As a preverbal child, I was vulnerable, innocent, and at the mercy of the adults who raised me. The abuse broke and violated my person. I was abandoned by my dad who was supposed to nurture, cherish, love, and care for me. I felt total rejection and complete disregard from him. The daily assaults of physical, verbal, and emotional attacks had annihilated my person and destroyed the ability to trust.

The fears I developed as a consequence of all of these factors carried over into my adult years. I became stubbornly self-reliant and felt shame in asking for help from another. Little did I know this was pride that resulted from shame. I was unable to receive assistance, even when I desperately needed it.

I had trouble accepting my feelings, regulating my emotions, and admitting my needs to anyone. I had difficulty feeling a sense of bonding and connection, even when I longed for intimacy. These feelings led to a sense of isolation, aloneness, fierce independence, and obstinate self-sufficiency. I struggled to have what I wanted: an intimate relationship with my husband and a closer connection with other women.

2. Love: I battled with the sense that "*I am unlovable.*" My dad continuously ignored me, and I never had one normal toned conversation with him. He never validated my feelings or spoke to me calmly. He never showed me anything except hatred, anger, and rage. When around him, my self-worth was zero, and I carried this belief that I was a nobody and unlovable into my adulthood. I had a shell of myself that existed, lacking the emotional resources and skills that should have been developing from early childhood. As a child, I could not differentiate my feelings or sort out the complexity of how I was treated poorly by my dad and unprotected by my mom who also became the target of his anger and rage.

Mistreatment only reinforced other beliefs attached to my feeling unlovable. I further believed I am not wanted. I will never be good enough in Dad's view; therefore, I felt no one would ever view me as worthy of love. I suffered as an adult with feelings of inadequacy and feeling completely inept at communicating emotions, developing close relationships, and making my way in a world I was unprepared to enter. I felt flawed and defected. I also had this sense that there was something very "*inherently wrong*" with me.

In adopting dysfunctional coping mechanisms, the only way I knew how to cope steered me into becoming a perfectionist, a people-pleaser, with an inability to say "no" and an unknowing in how to express how I felt about any subject or topic confidently.

I was unable to establish healthy boundaries, which affected my social relationships. Underlying all interactions with anyone was a constant vigilance and monitoring that occurred when I interacted with another; *they think I am an idiot; they view me as unworthy; they see me as unable; they think I am incompetent.*

It was usual for me to walk around, feeling like I was in a prison where I fearfully and timidly peered out at the world from behind bars. I built these walls as defenses to protect myself from ever being harmed again by anyone.

These thoughts that became profoundly rooted personality traits made me feel that I would never be accepted, no matter what I did. It was like I was on high alert (hypervigilant) to prepare myself for the coming rejection of anyone I became vulnerable with, so I hid my insecurities. I hid these feelings that I had something inherently "wrong" with me to the point I believed I was a failure at life. Even though a high achiever and I gained recognition for these, they never filled this gaping hole of feeling something was "missing."

3. Safety: *In my view, the world and others were dangerous and threatening.* Living in this hypervigilant fear state created hyperarousal. This hypervigilant state sent false sensory data to my brain, interfering with its standard processing of information about my internal and external environments. The world I lived in and the world I saw was a dangerous place that threatened any sense of well-being. I could not muster any rationale in my internal realm when it repetitively sounded alarming signals that *"something bad is about to happen."*

This feeling only increased my already high alert state into being overly controlling when trying to protect my children and myself from this *"bad thing that I knew was going to happen."* To me, there was no escaping the horrors of these thoughts that *"something bad"* was going to take place in some future period. I often awakened to this sense of *foreboding gloom and doom*, waiting in anxious anticipation for this bad "thing" to come looming disastrously into my world, crushing and breaking into my life. My behaviors and motivations became dictated by these unfounded fears, insecurities, increasing feelings of helplessness, and overwhelming anxiousness.

Any changes I wanted to make or habits I tried to alter and meet new people caused unease, discomfort, and a real point of tension and internal pain for me. Personal interactions required confidence and assurance I lacked. Even though I was a high-achieving person, motivated by a strong drive to succeed, no matter how hard

I tried or the many attempts I made to change, I could not, with any assurance, maintain stable or substantial changes.

I lacked the sense of feeling like a complete and integrated woman. My irritated anxiety, moody depression, and isolated aloneness caused me to be inaccessible and prevented others from accessing me. Seemingly carrying an indifference attitude, distancing myself from vulnerable conversations were traits that did not draw others towards me; instead, I was unconsciously pushing others away. People were unable to penetrate the walls of my defenses, and the barriers I constructed from adopting dysfunctional coping mechanisms and layers of pride that became impenetrable, even from God.

> For those who feel their lives are a grave disappointment to God, it requires enormous trust and reckless, raging confidence to accept that the love of Jesus Christ knows no shadow of alteration or change. When Jesus said, "Come to me, all you who labor and are heavy burdened," he assumed we would grow weary, discouraged, and disheartened along the way. These words are a touching testimony to the genuine humanness of Jesus. He had no romantic notion of the cost of discipleship. He knew that following him was as unsentimental as duty, as demanding as love.

> —Brennan Manning

Reflective encouragement

Trust, love, and safety are essential traits necessary to bond and connect with others. At age nineteen, encountering Jesus as a reality and experiencing the purest of lovers for the first time in my life was a stunning awakening. Due to experiencing childhood trauma, my life, even as a Christian woman was, at times, much of a struggle.

When I was finally able to receive the fullness of Jesus's love, I came to a more robust impression that, with his help, he could construct new understandings and new ideas from his transformative power. These new understandings flowed from life in Christ. Suffering, pain, and difficulties are now viewed through the lens of love.

You, too, can avail yourself of this same love. God's love is the transformative agent who will empower you to do this same work when choosing to trust him. The wholeness and integration resulted from love doing its perfect work, releasing me from the oppression of emotions controlling and ruling. In Christ, I was no longer bound under condemnation and judgment from violence. In Christ, my thoughts became untangled and restructured according to his thoughts, his sincerity, his genuineness. In Christ, the authenticity and power of agenda-free love, loosed, liberated and freed me from the past. In Christ, his holy perspective shaped mine. In Christ, love altered my focus and redirected my vision to his. In Christ, his love renovated from the inside-out. In Christ, the fire of his love were signs of his promised seal of the Holy Spirit whose filter I now see through.

> When I trust deeply that today God is truly with me and holds me safe in a divine embrace, guiding every one of my steps I can let go of my anxious need to know how tomorrow will look, or what will happen next month or next year. I can be fully where I am and pay attention to the many signs of God's love within me and around me.

> —Henri Nouwen

Will you consider joining me in this journey of receiving and discovering God's love?

You, too, can discover God's love as the key to releasing you from the bondage of the hurts and trauma of the past.

7

FORWARD MOMENTUM

Then Jesus turned to the Jews who had claimed to believe
in him. If you stick with this, living out what I tell you,
you are my disciples for sure. Then you will experience
for yourselves the truth, and the truth will free you.

—John 8:32 (MSG)

The Webster Dictionary definition of *acknowledging* is "*to admit
the existence or truth of a certain situation.*" It also means "*to express,
in recognition of noticing or becoming aware, that the situation is real.*"

In reality, when needing to change, alter, or modify habits, attitudes, careers, or relationships, one must first be aware of a need to change. Then one must be able to acknowledge what needs to change. Then one must be truthfully honest with themselves. I could not make any changes in my often-destructive behaviors and maladaptive coping mechanisms until I could fully recognize the interconnection in how these behaviors caused negative issues in my marriage, parenting, and other relationships.

The truth was something I tried to push down, ignore, or deny each time my husband brought my behaviors to my attention.

In receiving the wondrous love from Jesus, I could no longer live under the veil of denial and refusal to acknowledge my harmful actions towards others. I could no longer allow myself to continue in the same damaging and dysfunctional patterns. I had to admit my need to choose a *different response* to change and modify how I acted out the hurt and rage on those I cared about the most.

In selecting the courageous steps necessary to move forward, I recognized I had to take a different course of action to obtain different results. I began to feel a burning sensation stirring within my entire being, which was the beginning of feeling hopeful.

This tiny spark of *hope* helped me to trust in God's ability to help me do the mechanical part to change and to allow him entry inside to do this supernatural transformative work. I placed my little faith and that tiny seed of hope in the possibility of what could happen when trusting God. I chose to follow the potential of where he could take me. An *optimism* rose within me that his love could transform me to become the woman I often dreamed about in my mind—*untethered and free!*

Hope can help us find meaning and purpose in our lives, no matter the difficult struggles. The following excerpt was written by Dr. Paul T. P. Wong, who has suffered much in his life raised in China under the Mao Zedong regime and is often stigmatized due to his Asian heritage.

Paul T. P. Wong is a Canadian clinical psychologist and professor. His research career has gone through four stages with significant contributions in each stage: learning theory, social cognition, existential psychology, and positive psychology. This writing came from a period when Dr. Wong was confined to a hospital bed with cancer.

What is the meaning of life when you are confined to a room or a bed and struggling with every breath?

What is the point of living when so many people are dying and you may not see another sunrise?

Is life nothing more than just breathing?

More than mere feeding and elimination?

More than being kept alive by machines?

These questions kept me awake even when my body needed sleep. The answers came to me in a lucid dream.

Several old friends smiled at me, reminding me of the good time together, they came from different period of time.

I recalled the exciting moments, of my first degree, first love, first job, and what I had done for others.

I remembered the happy day, when I first heard God's call and many answered prayers.

Most of the meaningful moments, were hidden deep in my memory, and filled my heart with tears and joy.

The meaning of life can be found, in those precious moments and, the knowledge that I am not alone.

—According to Viktor Frankl and Dr. Paul TP Wong, *Made for Resilience & Happiness: Effective Coping with COVID-19,* pg. 69

I well remember them, and my soul is downcast within me. Yet this I call to mind and therefore I have hope: Because of the LORD's great love, we are not consumed, for his compassions never fail. They are new every morning; great is your faithfulness. (Lamentations 3:20–23 NIV)

Hope

In Webster's Online Dictionary, *hope* is the feeling that something wanted or desired can happen.

Upon awakening one particular morning, a sense of anticipation quickened my mind, body, and spirit. The day my life took a drastic shift, I thought I could make the changes necessary with God's help. Then the name of a therapist I had seen a couple of times, many years before, flashed in my mind. This psychologist was a believer in Christ, and this fact helped me put confidence that the divine power of God could work through him. The Holy Spirit prompted me to get in touch with him and set up an appointment. To me, this was my last chance and my final opportunity to obtain substantial changes.

After taking this step, I experienced several emotions hitting me all at once. *I felt desperate and scared. I felt helpless and overwhelmed. I doubted I could get the help needed.*

For the first time in my life, I permitted these emotions, feelings, and sensations to rise to the surface. I did not try to distance myself from them. I did not try to push them away. I did not try to run from them or deny them.

I welcomed and allowed them to exist. I invited these emotions to be just what they were: expressions. They were neither right nor wrong, good or bad.

Before my first meeting with this therapist, I was still a bit skeptical. I recognized my fears and asked God to help this psychologist, this man of faith, help me. I placed the tiny bit of trust I mustered in God, switching my focus from my inadequacies, choosing to rely on him to work through this man.

Hope had stirred a significant change in my mindset, and this occurred when I put my faith and trust in God to be the power and source to work through this man.

We need hope as much as we need light in the
darkest night. We need hope as much as we need air

to stay alive. Therefore, choose to believe in hope. As long as there is hope, everything is possible:

- *Hope drives away fear and anxiety.*
- *Hope rises above despair and depression.*
- *Hope overcomes all obstacles and enemies.*
- *Hope enables you to endure hardships and pain.*
- *Hope opens your eyes to discover that there is something in life that is worth fighting for.*
- *Hope awakens your soul to see the beauty, goodness, and truth in a cruel world.*
- *Hope always says yes to life and no to death.*

Science has shown that optimism is the most powerful motivation for us to move forward and maintain our mental health. The vital role of hope in preserving one's wellbeing and health has been well-documented (Snyder, 2000). It is difficult to conceive how we can maintain hope and confidence in the face of bleak prospects without faith, be it religious faith, trust in others, or self-confidence. In short, one cannot survive without faith or belief.

Once you lose faith in yourself or in humanity, you will be overwhelmed by waves of hopelessness and helplessness, which will make you more vulnerable to depression or suicide.

Faith enables you to attempt the impossible and take the first step to embark on a long and dangerous journey. A person of faith is a person of unshakable confidence and unwavering determination.

Tolstoy wrote "Faith is the sense of life, that sense by which man does not destroy himself, but continues to live on. It is the force whereby we live."

Therefore, do not lose faith in your own agency, in humanity, or in God. As long as you keep the faith and believe in hope, you will be unstoppable. Yes, everything is possible with faith and hope. We need all kinds of hope to fully benefit from its power.

—According to Viktor Frankl and Dr. Paul TP Wong, *Made for Resilience & Happiness: Effective Coping with COVID-19*, pg. 54

Hope aided me to believe with God, not only would changes be possible, but the lasting transformation I desired might also be possible. This was hope and optimism rising from the shattering of what trauma did to me.

According to Viktor Frankl, "*Between stimulus and response, there is a space. In that space is our power to choose our response. In our response lies our growth and our freedom.*"

Honesty

The goal of such instruction is love—the love that comes from a pure heart, a good conscience, and sincere faith. (1 Timothy 1:5 KNT)

As a Christian, learning to be *honest* with me, my husband, and before God was startlingly life-altering. Over the years, my husband tried to make me see the truth about how my destructive behaviors affected him. Although I acknowledged this, for me, it seemed more than difficult to change these behaviors, a seemingly insurmountable task. I kept running up against the obstacles of traumatic-driven energies. These energies seemed beyond my capability and capacity of breaking through with any sort of success.

On this day, my encounter with the reality of God's love moved me to a place I could no longer hide from these truths. I had to admit my role for the harm and damage I caused in my marital relationship like never before. I could no longer bury myself under a shroud of pretense.

Once I faced these truths, I felt a sudden surge of God's love saturating, filling, drenching, embracing, and empowering. His passion helped me take this critical step in admitting my failures courageously. What followed was that I allowed shame, guilt, fears, and negative emotions to rise.

I simultaneously released and let go of these emotions as God's love came rushing, gushing, and pouring into me. I was lifted by a divine presence whose warmth caringly held this tattered woman so close to a love I knew was real, authentic, and accurate. I did not turn or run away from the path God was leading me toward—his heart. I no longer denied my dire need.

I realized my greatest need was to respond and receive Christ and his love at this moment.

Over time, my beliefs began to shift and change from despairing ones to truths that strengthened. The Lord's love glimmered light, hope, honesty, and life into my world. The passion of Christ's love moved in a power unknown prior. Bit by bit, his love altered my inadequacies into secured assurance and trusted confidence in the sufficiency of God.

Freedom in truth

The Webster Dictionary definition of *acknowledging* is "*to admit the existence or truth of a certain situation.*" It also means "*to express, in recognition of noticing or becoming aware, that the situation is real.*"

Jesus revealed to me truths I could not obtain through this decision alone or by intellect or reason. The truth he unveiled was that the central focus, the central theme, and the central object of my faith and source of power for doing this courageous work was the person of Jesus Christ. His love showed me I needed to draw upon his ever steady and present grace.

How can I have the nature of Jesus? By being born from above, by the Holy Spirit coming into me on the ground of the Redemption and putting into me the disposition of Jesus. It is all done by the miracle of God's grace.

—Oswald Chambers, *Truth & Grace A Holy Pursuit*

Reflective encouragement

The way you and I view God will define how we consider ourself, others, and life. If we have a twisted understanding of God, our perceptions towards others and the world will be twisted also. This tiny spark of hope helped me to trust and receiving the truth of God's love. His love gave me the courage to do the mechanical part where I willingly allowed Jesus and his love entry inside to do this supernatural transformative work. I placed my tiny seed of hope in the possibility of what could happen when trusting God. Openly receiving the truth in Christ's love and drawing upon his grace helped me overcome a lifetime of wounds. His love is the genuine, authentic, and real power that made what I viewed as an impossible and insurmountable task *possible!*

The revealing truth in God to live a vibrant, meaningful, and intentional faith can only be discovered in the person of Jesus Christ. As my life became hidden in his glory and splendor, courage was emboldened, confidence inspired, and faith reignited. Working through trauma's bad stuff was more than possible when drawing upon the endless and matchless grace of Jesus.

You, too, can choose to follow the potential of Christ in you as you are bound in him. Christ inspires us with *optimism* to trust his love is more than able to transform you and me into the person we often dream about—*untethered and free!*

8

Necessary Processes

It is God who is at work in you, enabling you both
to will and to work for his good pleasure. Do all
things without murmuring and arguing.

—Philippians 2:13–14

Why are processes important? They are important because they
describe how things are done and prioritize steps to take and how to
apply one's mind and body with a focused intentionality. Not only are
these processes and steps vital, but having a proper attitude in going
through these measures are important. If we can learn how to mechanically process life challenges, integrating the good and bad events along
with incorporating both light and dark emotions, we will discover the
Lord's grace is enough to enable the transformation needed and wanted.

The only way to move beyond the systemic effects of trauma
and leave my past behind was to go through the following process:
acknowledging, accepting, and allowing.

1. Acknowledge the abuse that happened (truth is your
    companion).
2. Admit that trauma caused horrific consequences (truth is
    your dearest friend).
3. Accept what happened in its entirety (truth is your ally).

4. Allow, welcome, and invite these truths and your feelings (notice them, sit with them, listen to them).

Acknowledging

Before arriving at this place in my life, where I recognized the truth, *I felt lost; I felt shame; I felt deep-seated guilt; I felt crazy. I felt beyond hope.* I had been running away from God as my source of help. I had been running away from my husband's love and caring compassion. I had been running away from my feelings, viewing them as the enemy, denying and trying to hide them.

I had been running away from how the internalized messages and lies from the trauma became stored in my bodily system, forming a distorted identity.

I finally took responsibility and became accountable for accepting my role in the damage I had caused in my marriage and my life. I saw the reality of my need to change; *I stopped running.*

These forbidden truths came to the surface of my pained existence slowly, bit by bit, hitting me like a ton of bricks one morning, and I felt myself starting the long slow climb out of the *pit of hell.* When I eventually became honest in acknowledging how the consequences of the abuse caused turmoil and chaos in my life, a profound strength rose within me.

This strength came as I drew upon the supreme grace in Christ.

The beginning of my journey and the beginning of a lifelong transformation was discovered in a God whose love lavished upon me a spectacular grace. His spirit led me to develop practices where I gained self-discipline.

In taking an in-depth cold hard look at my life and viewing what I had become. I became acutely aware I had to make different choices to become someone other. After years of unsuccessful therapeutic interventions (before contacting the other professional mentioned earlier in this book), I became disillusioned, discouraged, and disappointed in professionals. At the beginning of entering therapy, I thought it would help me find an improved life. But after several years, I only felt myself spiraling further down the dark cyclical pit of what I came to view as a *"nightmarish torturous hell."* I found myself miserably stuck in a cold dark black hole—the sinking cavity of depression.

Yet, on that brave day, I allowed, invited, and welcomed these truths to rise to the surface of my awareness.

I realized I had placed an *excessive* amount of my trust and faith in others and in this professional instead of in the person of Jesus Christ whose power was the only source able to help.

> God can do anything, you know—far more than you could ever imagine or guess or request in your wildest dreams! He does it not by pushing us around but by working within us, his Spirit deeply and gently within us. (Ephesians 3:20 MSG)

Taking this brave step forward in facing my fears aided in putting to death the past lies (it was fear that hindered—fear of what other's thought, fear of being judged, fear of speaking truthfully, fear of vulnerability, fear of this and fear of that).

The processes I incorporated are ones you must go through to untangle the web of what abuse did to you. These processes required me to dig deeper into receiving the Father's love and drawing upon his provision of grace in Christ. His divine power disentangled and deconstructed the deception, the lies, the false beliefs, and the distorted truths I had come to believe as my version of reality. His love dismantled the fear-based foundation I knew and rebuilt, from the inside-out process, a firm foundation upon his love.

Acceptance

What naturally followed acknowledging was the necessity of fully accepting my emotions, the guilt from past actions, and the shame of who I had become. I had to make an active decision to stop resisting the Holy Spirit. I had to take the little bit of trust, I sensed, in not only accepting God's love as my help but in willingly receiving it.

I had to choose the act of purposefully and repetitively redirecting my thoughts towards God. I had to shift my priorities to choose to wholeheartedly and fervently pursue love as my way of life. I saw God as the only source who would help me stop the cycle of abuse. I learned bit by bit the art of yielding to the Holy Spirit *dysfunctional thought patterns, stubborn resistance, unhealthy attitudes, raw emotions, out-of-control behaviors, and pride.*

Implementing this process with each emotion with each issue and each obstacle I faced helped slow down my thoughts. I was guided by an internal source whose name is Jesus. His voice directed me to pay attention to what was happening. His love spirit helped me monitor my personal internal repertoire.

It was an inside-out journey full of *unexpected rewards, intense struggles,* and *vibrant renewal.* The path towards a relationship in Christ was the path in learning the art of surrendering resistances. I discovered I could trust God, and it began with choosing to believe his love over the lies.

The most significant and profound renewal that took place was the renewal of God's love life in mine. Renewed spiritual growth followed as a new life pattern. God's love began to reconnect, restore, and rebuild a healthier relationship in him, with me, and then with others.

God's spiritual renovation began to transform my perceptions, beliefs, and understanding of who I was at the base of my identity. Step by step, I traveled through the *"hell"* of what my life was at that time in rebuilding and retraining my thoughts and mind from the ground up. This method of inviting and welcoming my feelings as allies, as close friends and willing them to tell their story became a critical step in this moving forward process.

Allowing

I can recall the day I came to view as the end of self-rule and the decades restlessly spent battling an incurable mental illness, DID. I can clearly remember that morning as a reset in my life and the start of making choices *intentional.*

The choice to practice disciplines of my faith (prayer, reading scriptures, worship) and continuing to receive God's lavish love became my new pattern. I often sang the song that I wanted to "*surrender all*" to Jesus. Still, the barriers, obstacles, and walls that developed from what abuse had done to me hindered and prevented me from letting go to receive his love.

I came to understand that "*letting go*" involved a more profound understanding of accepting my inability and surrendering my helplessness to the reign of Christ. I recognized there must be an openness and a willingness to invite and welcome him inside the raging storm of emotional instability.

I became aware of my need to stop resisting the Holy Spirit. I needed to open my mind and soul to permit love to have unlimited access to every area of my life, holding nothing back.

Each day offered opportunities to make choices that were intentional ones that helped me link my life with Christ's. As I became more spiritually attuned and intentional in relating with love, in love, and by love, love cut the chains I was bound in. God's spirit poured in a steady flowing stream of abundant holy grace.

The day I came to the end of myself was the day I came face-to-face with the God whose presence was the real power that lifted me out of my plight. That day, I grew in trusting. I had faith, but I needed to understand I could trust Christ to lead me safely to the sacred dwelling place of the Father's heart where true love resided.

Reflective encouragement: The path towards accepting God's love, a self, life, and reality means we must stop holding onto the false truth (fears, distorted beliefs, deceptions, wrong assumptions), *surrendering "all"* to Jesus. Easy to say but much harder to do. This is more than possible in the realm of the divine and the holy. Dealing with the heavyweight of all the "stuff" (hurts, wounds, shame, guilt) and living from his provision of grace as our source is how you and I abide as new creations as God's people.

God never forces a person's will into surrender, and he never begs. He patiently waits until that person willingly yields to him. True surrender is a matter of being "united together [with Jesus] in the likeness of his death" (Romans 6:5) until nothing ever appeals to you that did not appeal to him. And after you surrender—then what? Your entire life should be characterized by an eagerness to maintain unbroken fellowship and oneness with God.

—Oswald Chambers

9

UNLOCKING YOUR SELF-IMPOSED PRISON

It's in Christ that we find out who we are and what we are living for. Long before we first heard of Christ and got our hopes up, he had his eye on us, had designs on us for glorious living, part of the overall purpose of working out in everything and everyone. It's in Christ that you, once you heard the truth and believed it (this Message of your salvation), found yourselves home free—signed, sealed, and delivered by the Holy Spirit. This signet from God is the first installment on what's coming, a reminder that we'll get everything God has planned for us, a praising and glorious life.

—Ephesians 1:11–14 (MSG)

Trust in Webster's online dictionary is defined as "*having reliance on the integrity, strength, ability, surety, etc., of a person or thing; confidence; confident expectation of something.*"

Expanding on what happened when I woke on that particular morning, I walked downstairs from another sleepless, restless night, falling onto the floor in utter exhaustion, crying out to the God I longed to know. I collapsed, having no energy, no strength, and no means to continue this cyclical madness. At that moment, I gave my entire self in melted surrender to God's love.

I let go of my intense wanting to resist and felt a loosening and unhinging. I sensed a breaking and an opening as I wholeheartedly placed my trust in God.

This crumbling released the key that shattered the walls of my defenses and allowed me to receive God's love. Love embalmed my fears and the emotions I had tried to run from—*shame, hurt, anger, rage.*

Faith in action

> Faith for my deliverance was not faith in God.
> Faith means whether I am visibly delivered or not,
> I will stick to my belief that God is love.

> —Oswald Chambers

What does it mean to trust God?

As adults, when we sit in a seat, we don't wonder if it will hold us; we trust that we are secured in the chair when we sit. This knowing is kind of how trust works. We have full confidence that chairs, sofas, and seats will hold us when we sit down.

Do you ever question when you sit on a chair whether it will fail you or crumble beneath you? Over time, I bet you never doubt whether chairs will fulfill the function they were meant to do. You trust when you sit, the chair will hold you, and you will not fall to the ground.

The same idea can be considered when trusting God. Trust is a gradual process in developing, but over time, as we experience the security of God's love, we discover the Father is goodness, mercy, and rightness. We arrive in this same sense when trusting him, knowing that he is faithful to do all he has promised and is worthy of our trust. We have experienced his grip upon us, and we have experienced the transforming power and touch of his love working in and through our human frame.

Imagine God's love as sitting in a chair. Now imagine the chair as God's heart and imagine him holding you and caring for you from that place. God's strength, compassion, kindness, mercy, and true love are firmly rooted in you as the chair. His passion is flowing into you, inside you, filling every space in your body. It will be the entity that forever changes who you are and whose you are. Father will never fail in what he has promised. He promised to be with you and me always, constantly, assuring us he will be our steady source of help when we call upon the name of his Son, Jesus.

The more you allow and willingly open your mind and heart to experience his warmth and genuine care, the more you will learn you can trust his love and that he has the best plans in store for you, *even in dark times*. The most challenging time to see God's agenda is when everything seems to be falling apart. We often do not understand God's plans amid suffering and pain, but we can know the truth—his plans include goodness and love. We can trust and learn that his plans cannot be hindered or prevented from proceeding in his watchful care and holy pursuit. God's life flourishes, even from horrific life circumstances and tragedy *(Genesis 50:20; Isaiah 14:27, 46:10–11; Psalms 33:11; Jeremiah 29:11).*

God is not concerned about our plans; he doesn't ask, "Do you want to go through this loss of a loved one, this difficulty, or this defeat?" No, he allows these things for his own purpose. The things we are going through are either making us sweeter, better, and nobler men and women, or they are making us more critical and fault-finding, and more insistent on our own way. The things that happen either make us evil, or they make us more saintly, depending entirely on our relationship with God and its level of intimacy.

—Oswald Chambers

Here are a few helpful suggestions to consider

1. Take Responsibility for my actions, even when afraid.
2. Intentionality—be purposeful about where I am focusing *(Hebrews 12:2).*
   A) Trust, *even when my feelings don't match.*

B) Believe God's truth, *even when I don't feel like it.*

C) Cultivate trust, *even when insecure.*

D) Surrender to the Spirit of love, *even when I don't want to.*

E) Let go of resistances (pride, stubbornness, arrogance), *even when I fear.*

F) Trust God over anything or anyone as my source of help, *even when I don't understand.*

Trusting in God means more than words written on the page

When I first encountered God's love at age nineteen and then again after a lifetime of struggling, I knew without a doubt, this was real and authentic love. I knew no matter what happened in my life, he would always be in and with me, never leaving me alone, *even when I did not feel his presence.*

I grew in my ability to trust his promise that I was a new creation and that my *need* was choosing to live from his divine nature.

Trust means that I am assured and confident that my Father will perform what he promises. Faith means I know he will remain the One to fulfill his promises, *according to his perfect plans and purposes.* I don't wonder or question his love for me or others as I am secure in his passion.

Trust in God means giving up my wanting to control, fix, or solve this "thing." Trust is consenting for God to do the necessary transformation in my life or in others, *even when I fear, doubt, or don't understand.*

Trust is faith in action and requires me to let go of my tendency to act or react from a flesh stance and intentionally choose to co-participate with the Spirit. Trust believes God's grace is sufficient to aid me in all hardships, in every circumstance, and in each relational difficulty. Trust is known confidence in God that whatever life event I am experiencing might not change. Still, looking to Father in my circumstances, my heart attitude must and will become transformed.

Trust is knowing when I partake of his divine nature—Jesus Christ promises *grace for the moment, the hour, the day.*

Trust lets me know Father always responds to me and others in mercy and love. Trust knows he has the best plans in store for me and you and us as a community of saints and that they are right and good. Trust believes Father leads in peace by reconciling and redemptive love.

Trust in his love caused me to reformulate my perception of God, self, and life from the center of his heart as truth. Trust meant believing scriptures were more than words written on a page. These words described Father's nature and character. They were full of spiritual manna, feeding my soul, body, and spirit, birthing new life from the remnants of the past.

Trust is "seeing" the revelation of his promises to be accurate, such as in Jeremiah 29:11, *"For I know the plans I have for you" (NIV)*.

Trusting is knowing that God has divine plans, even in the hardest of times and in the tumultuous of battles. Trust is knowing that I will benefit spiritually (Romans 8:28), *no matter what "things" appear.*

It took many years to realize God was the Father I never had and the Father I needed, wanted, and could fully trust. On that day in the shattering, I received the fullness of his majestic love, and there was an unreserved agreeing and granting of my will to him.

Receiving his love gave me the courage to dig into human resilience and leave behind the shame, guilt, and fears. Accepting his love helped me move into the reign of Christ's life. His life allowed me to live beyond my trauma and to finally leave my past in the dust. Living from this love's revelation is trusting Christ to do his miraculous work from the inside-out. Trust is knowing his passion disarms the lies. His love softens flesh-tendencies. His love melts pride. His love exchanges self-reliance with renewed hope, light, and life.

God offers grace to live a faith measured in love

3. Holy Spirit empowers
   A) Respond in allowing God's love entry, *even when prideful.*
   B) Willingly listen and discern the Lord's voice *over cultural, societal, familial, and religious representatives.*

C) Trust God's truth *over the lies, religious systems, cultural mores, societal standards, opinions of others, and voices from the past.*

I'm glad in God, far happier than you would ever guess—happy that you're again showing such strong concern for me. Not that you ever quit praying and thinking about me. You just had no chance to show it. Actually, I don't have a sense of needing anything personally. I've learned by now to be quite content whatever my circumstances. I'm just as happy with little as with much, with much as with little. I've found the recipe for being happy, whether full or hungry, hands full or hands empty. Whatever I have, wherever I am, I can make it through anything in the One who makes me who I am. (Philippians 4:10–14 MSG)

As I reflected on the meaning of the above passage, the critical views I was very familiar with rose their voices clamoring: *I can't, I am not able, no way can I make it. No way can I change. God is not going to help me.*

God's love affirmed, *"I am the plan. I am the change. I am who I am. I am guidance. I am power. I am life. I am love."*

4.   Confront false thoughts as deceptions.

God spoke tender words, *"If you want a new life, let me into your heart, mind, and soul. Become intentional. In me, you can take hold of these disabling thought patterns and choose a new way to think. I will perform these changes. Yet, you must be a willing participant and allow yourself to receive me into your inner world and in an ongoing manner.*

You must wholeheartedly give every inch of yourself to me. Let my life think, dwell, and breathe inside the walls and secret hidden spaces. I am spirit-being-life. I am love. I cradle and hold you near and am lib-

erty and freedom. I am truth, light, and hope. I will speak, and you will hear and know my voice. Choose to respond from my love instead of your emotions and fears. I am your hope, dearest companion, closest friend, and trusted confident."

I questioned and doubted. I asked myself, how will this happen? How will I do this? How will I become different? Will he really help me change and be who he created me to grow into my God-identity?

I immediately heard the Lord's assurance, *"Each morning, I invite you to put aside all other tasks and come spend alone time in and with me. You must find a space where you will not be distracted or interrupted by anything or anyone else. I want you to open scriptures and read. I will give wisdom and insight, instructing and leading you in prayer and worship. I will teach you my ways, and from my perspective, I will lead you deeper in love. My love and heart will be with you always."*

God knew that my thoughts needed restructuring, so his first role was to help ground and order my mind. The truths of who God is and who he says I am are found in Christ. He produced confidence and empowerment that flowed from Christ. In Christ, I was secured and anchored to a love that assured.

The Father strengthened my weak belief with sound promises: *"Trust me, your* LORD *with all your heart and lean not on your understanding; in all your ways submit to me, and I will make your paths straight"* (Proverbs 3:5–6 NIV).

My heart immediately and unreservedly responded with, "Yes, *yes, and yes! I desire, long and want you. I will trust you to be the one to teach me and lead me closer to your love. I will not turn back, and I will never leave you. No matter the results or what matters of change occur and no matter what happens, I will follow you for the rest of my days on earth."*

As tears flowed unashamedly and in gut honesty, I pleaded for God to forgive me for looking to other sources for help. I asked him to create a new life from the mess of mine. I asked him to help me grow in godly attitudes and healthy habits. I asked him to lead me into his love as a lifestyle and way of being.

When I got up from the floor, wiped the tears from my face, I heard the Holy Spirit say, *"I will lead you into the spiritual truths of my kingdom. I will guide you nearer to Father's love. Begin now, this moment. Sit in the green lounge chair and open your bible and start reading. I want you to first thing every morning, go downstairs, sit in this chair, and open your Bible. Don't pay attention to your emotions or feelings or if you slept.*

"Don't place a great deal of focus on the other thoughts that will come to you. Ignore the racing thoughts and emotions that overwhelm. Just sit down and read, soak in my words and the concepts written in scriptures. I will give you insights, and I will take you into a more profound, more comprehensive, and broader expanse of my fullness. Do not focus on results, but redirect your attention to my spirit, my voice, my love."

His still small voice encouraged me, ordering my thoughts according to the truth: *"Be strong and courageous. Do not be afraid or terrified because of them, for the* LORD *your God goes with you; he will never leave you nor forsake you"* (Deuteronomy 31:6–8 NIV).

This particular passage in Scriptures had been one of my go-to verses over the years and one I had heard and learned in my early beginnings as a Christian at age nineteen. The meaning of that verse began to shape my life. I understood that this was who Father was, and he was more than just words on a page. These were love promises encouraging, supporting, and abiding inside as *strengthened renewed life.*

Overcome by the Spirit, I then sat in the green recliner chair and eagerly heard his steady voice, *"I live inside you each moment of each hour of each day. There will not be one second you will ever be alone or without my life. Trust me over any person, any institution, religion, book, and other sources. I will be your God, and I will be the One whose love leads you in this process. You must let go of the result you think you want and place your entire trust in me, regardless of the outcome."*

At that moment, I put my trust in his love as an act of my will, *even though skeptical.*

The following scripture then came to mind, *"Create in me a pure heart, O God, and renew a steadfast spirit within me"* (Psalm 51:10).

These verses became my heartfelt prayer and mantra. As I read, meditated, considered, and reflected on scriptures, I earnestly prayed those words. In tears and brokenness, I embraced them as the Father embraced me right where I was—*a shattered woman.*

Understanding my need to choose *intentionality* as a lifestyle and willing to give my *"all"* to Jesus became a turning point in my spiritual quest and morning routines.

Today, upon awakening, my thoughts turn to God, thanking him for another day.

On warmer days, I sit on our enclosed front porch beside an open window, breathing in the air and listening to the birds chirping. I join the harmony of sound with my song, *"God, thank you for continuing your work in me as I learn to live from the new heart you have created in me. Continue feeding me from the height, breadth, and depth of Your love. I am grateful for the gift of your life in mine."*

Unless we form the habit of going to the Bible in bright moments as well as in trouble, we cannot fully respond to its consolations because we lack equilibrium between light and darkness.

—Helen Keller

Reflective encouragement

This process moves forward when we make the mechanical effort to put forth the determination and energy to do work. Then we learn to trust in the supernatural activity of a God whose love performs this miraculous life-altering transformation.

I still have days I feel a bit discouraged or sad. I don't always have ready solutions, answers, or remedies to the difficulties I experience. In my humanness, I accept my vulnerabilities and limitations.

Yet, in all seasons, tough and easy, I have come to realize, love is where I am to live, dwell, and reside. The love I need is the love I receive daily from a Savior who joins me in suffering, in pain and in sorrow. The love I need is the love I receive each moment from a Lord who delights in me, his beloved.

He grace is sufficiently supplied within the Father's heart of desired love. The Father bestows his offering and gift of Love upon each person and has provided us with a Lord who is acquainted with suffering. Father did not leave us alone, but gifts to all those who receive this love, the divine influence of the Holy Spirt, who empowers, teaches and leads us into authenticity of what it means to be human beings.

The Natural Heart does not want the Gospel. We will take
God's blessings and his loving-kindness and prosperity, but
when God's Spirit informs us that we have to give up the rule
of ourselves and let him rule us, then we understand what
Paul means when he says the 'carnal mind is enmity against
God.' the wonderful work of the grace of God is that through
the Atonement God can alter the center of my life, and put
there a supreme, passionate devotion to God himself.

—Oswald Chambers, *Truth & Grace A Holy Pursuit*

10

A GOD-DIRECTED STRATEGY

The world is unprincipled. It's dog-eat-dog out there! The world
doesn't fight fair. But we don't live or fight our battles that
way—never have and never will. The tools of our trade aren't
for marketing or manipulation, but they are for demolishing
that entire massively corrupt culture. We use our powerful God-
tools for smashing warped philosophies, tearing down barriers
erected against the truth of God, fitting every loose thought and
emotion and impulse into the structure of life shaped by Christ.
Our tools are ready at hand for clearing the ground of every
obstruction and building lives of obedience into maturity.

—2 Corinthians 10:3 (MSG)

One day, when reading Scriptures, this verse popped out of the
pages at me. I heard the Spirit say that I am not to depend on human
methods (self-made plans and looking to other sources) as my guide
to help me through the transformation God desired. God was leading me to adopt spirit-directed strategies to build a foundation based
on his love.

God showed me my human thoughts and methods were powerless strategies of this world. He revealed my need to smash distorted
beliefs in twisted and skewed truths from past trauma.

My mind was enlightened, and I recognized that only in the power of Father's love would the massive obstructions be removed from their lofty positions. Those entities that held me captive in the prison of "*hell*" those many decades were embedded into the core of who I had become.

The walls I built were fortresses that needed to be torn down and dismantled. These were the philosophies and knowledge that were rooted in abusive violence. The experience I assimilated were those of the perpetrator. The violent abuse was the vain philosophy that skewed and twisted my God-ordained identity. The offensive actions against me and the steel cage I hid behind resulted from years of endemic violence that had entirely shattered my ability to receive God's love.

The misuse of love and wrongly applied power of abuse entangled my heart in disbelief that God loved me—*the no strings attached kind of love.* Who I became from violence and trauma needed a complete overhaul. My life required reframing according to God's holy order and divine design.

My spiritual eyes awakened to what was needed. I willingly received God's invitation and trusted his affirming spirit of love. He led me in this process of disarming, demolishing, and removing the distorted roots from their lofty hold that confined me in spinning chaos and swirling darkness. His passion dethroned those principalities (stuck emotional rulers and controllers) and strongholds (lies, false beliefs, false perspective). It released a vulnerable, extravagant, generous, extravagant grace.

I) *Strongholds from the past*

Spiritual strongholds begin with a thought. One thought becomes a consideration. A consideration develops into an attitude, which leads then to action. Action repeated becomes a habit, and a habit establishes a "power base for the enemy," that is a stronghold.

—Elisabeth Elliot

1. Lies from the past. Discerning truth from lies gives good reason to gain biblical understanding. Believing in false facts imprisoned me in this spiraling downward spinning, out-of-control chaotic lifestyle. The messages I internalized and received as a preverbal child were the ones needing dismantling. It was those systems that needed complete reorientation according to divine truth where love reigned and ruled.

Father's lovelight helped me identify the numerous "false truths" and weed out the lies that formed those old false belief systems. These fraudulent messages damaged my perception of who I was at my core identity. In the breaking and the opening, Father led me to begin responding to his invitation to receive the gift of his most divine and holy love.

In practicing self-discipline, I reigned in obsessive, ruminating thoughts, aligning them to God-truth. I learned to replace those lies with divine realities that empowered and grounded me in confident-producing views and perceptions that flowed from a being whose origin was spirit-nature. Christ, in me, filled the tattered fabric of my soul, holding, washing, and redeeming my wounds, hurts, and suffering in transformative holy passion.

2. False beliefs that stemmed from these lies. *I was not good enough; I was unwanted. No one would accept me. I was a defect. I was a permanently flawed individual. I was unlovable by anyone, including my husband and God.*

In receiving the revelation of Christ's love and view, he renewed my beliefs according to his perspective from his divine nature as my new heart.

As my understanding matured through the lens of love, I discovered the truths of Father's perspective that I personally was his dearly loved and wanted Christ-one.

Father affirmed, "*You are my beloved, I delight in you, and I created you in love, by love, and for love. I loved you from before you were born. I loved you when you were in your mother's womb. My passions pursued you each second of each day from birth, even now and in each moment forward. I have redeemed, reconciled, and restored you to my passion. I am drawing you daily to this same love. You are holy, righteous, and completely forgiven. The heart you have been given is of divine origin and spirit-nature. I live in you, and you live in me, and we are joined with a never-ending love-union for all seasons and in all time."*

3. False perspective. My self-loathing prevented me from believing in the genuineness of another person's love, including God's. Those foundational messages (strongholds, lies,– false truths) were what needed to be destroyed, and my foundational base identity needed reforming based on Christ's transformative supernatural heavenly love.

Placing *trust* in God allowed me to *let go* of those strongholds of resistances—*scarred wounds, embittered hurts, hostile rage, guilted shame.* In opening and receiving this holy love to have unlimited access to my pained sorrows, God released a radical redeeming power showering me in his goodness and mercy in those places.

A supreme and sovereign influence deposited holy wisdom, reconstructing my views and perceptions according to the Spirit. The choice to trust and receive this love opened a new understanding of Jesus as a compassionate spirit-being who became my constant source of truth, hope, and life.

Once I made an active choice to stop resisting and opening myself to the bounty of Father's fullness, the floodgates of holy presence rushed in; saturating and drenching every nook, cranny, and fiber of my being in an unreserved and resolute love. His passion became the authoritative source that transformed my deep-seated false core beliefs into truth-empowering ones. This love-base created a converted perspective, where I began to view a self, God, and life through this divine filter as Christ's expressed nature.

4. Trust in other sources. I had to learn to exchange trusting in those other sources with trusting God, *even when my*

faith seemed small. I chose to live a lifestyle in trusting him, *even when I doubted and feared.*

Once I made the courageous decision to face the demons of my past, releasing fear, stubbornness, and pride, I received the expanse of God's immense all-consuming love. The reality, genuineness, sincerity, and authenticity of his spirit-being life became what I knew as truth. This revelation of true love whose power performed this work radically transformed me from the inside-out, overcoming the impossible.

I found I could rebuild a life in trusting God, slowly and bit by bit, turning over to his love fears, shame, and guilt. Trust began with believing him over my thoughts, emotions, lies, and religious perceptions from the past. As I chose to trust his love over anything or anyone else, the holy spirit poured in an empowered grace. I tapped into bravery and, in the act of courage, allowed love inside while choosing to *"let go"* of all I resisted; rage, hate, anger, fears, hurts, shame, and guilt (this happens over time).

God is the builder, and he is the Anointed One who lays the foundational pieces needed to restructure a healthy life. His love was the agent who cultivated courage that I could *"let go"* of the walls I used to push others away. The revelation of the breath of his love was the power I needed where I found I could learn to trust him, and I also realized I could begin to choose to trust other people too.

Never give up, for that is just the place
and time that the tide will turn.

—Harriet Beecher Stowe

Reflective encouragement

This process will take time, patience, and lots of hard work. In this process, I remained in an attitude of receptivity in receiving Christ's life as light, truth, and love. I responded to his passion in my weariness. In the shattering and breaking, love strengthened and helped me let go and receive all Father desired to give in his grace provision.

The key to receiving God's love was *letting go of my resistance. God released his promised provision of a grace that loosened and liberated.*

God proved to be *trustworthy* and *faithful* to fulfill what he promised. He performed the transformation I needed, wanted, and desired *as his precious loved one, created from love and for love.*

II) *Tearing down the walls (lies, distorted beliefs, skewed truths)*

1. I was learning to monitor internal dialogue. I had to stop listening to the cyclical bombarding disabling ideas. I had to shut them down immediately as soon as they popped into my head. I had to quickly end this thinking. I had to choose to become more aware of my internal conversations, discerning Father's love-voice among the chatter.

When I heard myself repeating lies in my head, I started confronting them with what I knew to be God-truth. As I delved into Scriptures, I began to see the realities of who God said I was and refused to listen to the false ideas. I started affirming what I believed as kingdom truths. I had to keep bringing my views of those lies into submission to what I knew the truth.

In regularity and with repetitive practice, this process became more manageable. Over time, my thoughts, ideas, and emotions became ordered, organized, and cohesively ordered according to Father's heart of light, truth, life, and love.

2. I was becoming intentional. I chose to think differently. I repeated to myself who God said I was. I wrote down relevant scripture passages to memorize, consider, reflect on, and incorporate into my thoughts.

The more I turned my concentration and focus on God's character and truths, the more the lies began to diminish. Over time and slowly, Christ's life altered thoughts and beliefs into confident-producing ones.

The revelation of Christ's love began to reformulate and transform my emotional thought patterns from distorted, unhealthy ones to life fostering empowering ones. And the radical transformation that occurred was in relating and viewing the self, others, experience, and God through the filter of Jesus's redemptive and healing love. Even in my skeptical mind, this change happened over time, just like Father promised.

3. I was learning to let go of resistance. This, too, became a necessary choice in this inside-out process. I realized that I could, with *God's power and help*, discipline my mind. As I willingly let go of the felt resistances, the more readily Father's being fullness and love began to fill in those reserved spaces and take root, just like he promised. This supernatural divine love's experiential reality began to flourish as the core foundational soundness in my mind, body, and spirit.

4. I was learning to accept responsibility. I chose to take action to change my thoughts. Each one of us can exercise *self-control* over thoughts. It is an act of our will to do this.

Restraint is also one of the fruits of the spirit listed in Galatians 5:22–23: *"But the fruit of the Spirit is love, joy, peace, patience, kindness, goodness, faithfulness, gentleness, self-control; against such things, there is no law."*

I had to be willing to admit that I could regain control of my thoughts with God's help.

You, too, can begin to choose to think, dwell, and redirect thought patterns towards God-conscious ones. You can select intentionality as a lifestyle and make faith-choices that align with God-truths. It results when you willingly choose to just do it.

As I put my faith into action in responding yes to God and no to the past, his love became the source and spiritual influence transforming. His activity entered the shattered girl of my childhood and began to rebuild my identity from the ground up. His passion restored and reconciled me as an adult woman to an expressively infinite spirit-being God.

5. I confronted faulty beliefs. My thoughts—not just my behavior—must change. I had to learn to work from the inside-out. Change begins with an internal process, going deeper into those places I forbid anyone entry, including myself. Father's love guided me to still my inner activity and listen, slowing down, attentively attuned in hearing, focusing, and disciplining my thoughts.

I chose discipline and self-control as habits. The deeper I delved into scriptures and lived from the infinite supply of Christ's life, the deeper I was experiencing divine order and holiness.

According to Scriptures, my behavior flowed outwardly from my thought patterns. As God's divine power transformed me through the *renewing* of my mind, my most potent medium was applying biblical models of truth (Romans 12:2).

6. I declared God's truth *over fear, false beliefs (lies), chaotic emotions, and holds of the past.* I willingly and determinedly grabbed hold of my disabling thoughts. I confessed that I neglected to seek God above any other source.

In Christ, I *"took captive every thought to make it obedient to Christ"* (Romans 12:21 KNT).

I boldly confronted my disabling thoughts and fears by naming them and facing them head-on. In naming them, I gradually turned them over one-by-one to Father. I began to see self, life, and relationships from a spiritual perspective. The spirit guided me to stop focusing on the old (past) and look at the new creation, which Father said I was in Christ *(2 Corinthians 5:17)*.

This process took a concerted effort and hard work to take my thoughts captive to God-truths. Each time a lie popped into my head, I stopped paying attention to them. I simply said *no* to thinking of them and chose to say *yes* to my heavenly Father. This process was more than possible. The personification of Christ's love revealed the living embodiment of his spirit-being. His divine source became my predominant mode of truth and transformation.

7. I acted from obedience, *even when I didn't feel like it.* Choosing obedience is possible even when my emotions are spinning wildly. In my traumatic-driven behaviors, obsessive thoughts and unstable feelings were what drove and motivated my living. Instead of letting them continue sabotaging my life, I learned to openly and willingly receive the Spirit of love to be the motivating agent in my inner realm.

The biblical model says when our emotions are ruling us, we become a double-minded person. A double-minded person is restless and confused in her thoughts, her actions, and her behavior. Such a person is always in conflict with herself.

The term *double-minded* comes from the Greek word *dipsuchos*, meaning "a person with two minds or souls."

In reading *James 1:8, 4:8*, the Spirit revealed that the trauma in my life caused me to doubt God's ability to help me. I then became this double-minded person spoken of in these passages, *conflicted in every area.*

The Spirit granted insight and opened my spiritual eyes to the treasures of Father's kingdom. I began living from the no-lack supply of Christ's reign as my way of being, trusting his love over the past. Each day, with repetitive practice, I responded with a yes to him as my endless love-source and a resounding no to the lies, emotions, shame, guilt, and the past as authoritative guides.

I accepted the invitation from Jesus to walk with him in the garden of my soul. I let the fragrance of his love breathe revival inside, and as a result, it was holy love who held me steadily near Father's heart.

What began as an act of my will towards obedience transformed into desire and an intense longing to spend time alone in God. I eagerly wanted to read Scriptures meditatively, absorbing life from those truths. The spirit prompted me to lift my voice, leading me in praise and worship. God drew me into long periods of interceding prayer. I began to want to replace my will and act from love as my source and response to living. What started as a disciplined effort became a natural instinct and by-product of godly love that flowed from me to the world.

8. I actively chose intentionality as a lifestyle as God's love redirected me to focus on the right things.

Paul writes in Philippians 4:8 what some things are "*true, noble, right, pure, lovely, and admirable.*"

As I began to redirect thoughts on God-truths, I refused to obsess about past matters, false beliefs, and distorted ruminating cycles.

Day by day, I chose intentionality as a lifestyle. I filtered what I allowed entry inside my thoughts, what I heard, saw, and read regarding conversations, TV, movies, magazines, social media, Internet, and written material. I dropped and let go of anything that did not produce life, peace, or joy.

Each day, I made a personal commitment not to give up when my thoughts tried to overtake and consume me. I dedicated time, paced efforts, and stood ground in responding from Christ's life, *even when overwhelmed.*

I retrained thoughts towards healthy connections (neuroplasticity) in building new neural pathways by focusing on sound biblical patterns centered on a being who is love.

In taking these actions, the Holy Spirit nurtured and cultivated divine love and holy order as a new way to think, respond, and be in my attitude. I readily accepted and received his love each day. Over time, I obtained newfound freedom to view God, myself, others, and life through his love-lens. Love inspired hope of Christ in me as manifestations of Father's light, truth, and grace.

9. Intentional choosing. I experienced severe challenges with conflicting and overwhelming thoughts. I stopped the negative thinking and overcame this battle with holy love as a divine source. How I viewed struggles and suffering changed, and I began to see them as opportunities to grow and mature in my understanding of grace.

My inner dialogue changed from, "*I can never do anything right*" to "*I can do all things through Christ*" *(Philippians 4:13).*

I believed in God's ability to do "*exceedingly, abundantly, above all according to his power which works in us*" (Ephesians, 3:12).

I let go of despair, hopelessness, and anger by taking control of what I could and *stopped* the monstrous lies in their tracks. I simply said *no* to them and responded with an absolute *yes* to the Spirit.

The revelation of Christ's life is he wants to pass through the tattered frame of my weakness and limited humanness. Christ offers grace in my vulnerabilities, and his presence wants to glorify Father in suffering and pain.

> I am, however, alive—but it isn't me any longer; it's the Messiah who lives in me. And the life I do still live in the flesh, I live within the faithfulness of the son of God, who loved me and gave himself for me. (Galatians 2:20 KNT)

My trust is in what Christ accomplished on the cross and the fact when I received Christ, my "sin" nature was put to death and existed no more. In Christ, God imparted divine spirit in me who now lived, thinking, and being life, liberty, and freedom in and through me. It is Jesus's faith within me that grows and matures faith.

God will continue to perform his love-work in transforming all I think, know, and am becoming. I trust his love as genuine and real. I believe him to live his life in and through mine as good, honorable, and holy.

It was in releasing and letting go of my resistances (unknowing, fears, doubts, anger, rage) and moving into the reign of Christ's life, his love was setting me free. Christ in me and me in him, intertwined in the blood of his life passing through my mind, renewed, refreshed, and revived. His life helped me overcame years of battling and struggling.

Galatians 2:19–20 is the picture of how you and I, as believers, are in an organic union with Christ. This union is formed through the divine origin and vulnerability of the Father's love. This occurred the moment I placed trust in Christ, receiving salvation. Salvation is the sanctifying and regenerating work of Christ's love/life. The day I received his free gift of salvation and each day moving forward, I live in, with and by grace.

At that moment, there is no longer any "sin" that separates me from the wholeness of his love and life *(John 14:20, 17:23; Romans 8:20; Colossians 1:27)*. Christian living is learning to simply respond from this life as the origin and source of energy. This union is the indwelling life of Father, Son, and Holy Spirit within the human. It is the mysterious union of their partnership and marriage in me; I am one in and with them as they are my sole source of sufficiency in all experiences, good and bad.

I was choosing a possibility. It is not easy to retrain wild thoughts or to respond according to the Spirit. I accepted the offer of living from the life of Christ as a viable alternative and godly influence.

What I had tried did not work, so why not try this option and possibility in Christ? I had nothing to lose and everything to gain by placing my frail belief in trusting him over those "things" and forces that held me in bondage.

I chose to step into his divine presence where a power higher than mine granted an inner capacity and bold resilience. Christ's love cut the chains that gripped me in bondage, revealing and releasing his passion in the spirit of freedom, liberty, life.

The more I practiced responding from love, the more I understood my need to be in the union with Christ so his spirit-life could manifest the Father. The more profound revelation was that Christ worked and performed lasting transformative and radical love in and through the suffering and pain I had endured. The greater miracle is

Christ in me is continuing to perform his radical love to bring glory to the Father.

> God has bestowed upon us, through his divine power, everything that we need for life and godliness, through these things, his precious and wonderful promises; and the purpose of all this is so that you may run away from the corruption of lust that is in the world, and may become partakers of the divine nature. (2 Peter 1:3 KNT)

There is no weakness in Christ, and we lack nothing required to live this faith. The manifestation of Christ's life became a natural by-product of his love, thinking, feeling, and relating outwardly to others from the joined union with his spirit blended in mine. I am no longer living in an isolated aloneness or detached sense from my own body. I am tightly grafted into the living vine. His life and love birthed authentic freedom and liberty that satisfied and fulfilled my deepest desire (John 15).

The roots of my thoughts, attitudes, and choices flow from Christ's very nature and origin. I am in the union as belonging to the life-blood of the vine. As a branch of God's family, the roots of all I am are in Christ as his blood flows through my cells, veins, and bodily systems. My thoughts, interests, activities, goals, pursuits, and choices now flow from Christ's claims, training, goals, and dreams. These are filtered through the love-will and higher purposes of the Father's plans.

Each of us can learn to develop a new view of who we are and see ourselves as a new creation when receiving God's divine and supernatural love. We do this by seeing life from God's perspective, based on our union in Christ, and remaining tightly intertwined and closely knitted in his life-blood as life (*John 15:4*).

As new creations, we have been deposited with the Son of God's very nature whose life we belong intimately interconnected to and with. The Father, Jesus Christ, and the Holy Spirit indwell as life, and we are gifted with a righteous, holy, God-nature. Embedded with the sacred, indwelling life, we are endowed with spiritual inclinations, godly desires, and divine attributes. The Spirit reveals, unveils, and unfolds God's kingdom treasures, gifts, and truths where faith is about learning to respond from our new hearts.

> Faith sees the invisible, believes the unbelievable,
> and receives the impossible.
>
> —Corrie ten Boom

Reflective encouragement

It is possible to live a life in allowing love to transform one's unhealthy inner dialogue and grab every thought taking it captive by God's power! God gave us unlimited access to the Holy Spirit who takes up residence inside our human frame. Jesus is the source and provision of divine spirit-being-life. Living from this limitless supply and his infinite life is my response to a holy love.

God promises to be with you and me and us as a community of believers every step along the way.

God is love, and love is greater than the forces from our past. God has infused his holiness, intertwining Christ's love life in ours, where his grace becomes all-sufficient (2 Corinthians 12:9). It is possible to overcome the consequences of abusive actions and the harm done to us as our life becomes hidden in Christ. His very life becomes our significant source of power, and we become intra-dependent in him as our *way of being.*

> There are certain points of truth Our Lord cannot reveal to us
> until our character is in a fit state to bear it. The discernment
> of God's truth and the development of character go together.
>
> —Oswald Chambers, *Truth & Grace: A Holy Pursuit*, pg. 105

Review

I started my healing journey, actively participating in acknowledging, accepting, and allowing. When I discovered the harmful messages and lies affected me, I found Christ's love was more than enough to combat those falsities.

When I was able to *name and identify the secret* of shame, there was a breaking and a lifting that released me from my past bondage. When I chose to open the door of my heart to trust in Christ, I allowed myself to trust his truth over all that I had known previously. I found the beginning of real freedom was discovered in the power of vulnerable and humble love.

I found I could receive the unlimited bounty of his continual streaming and outpouring of liberal love. I found when I stopped resisting and turned my attention to the things of the spirit, the layers of defenses began to shed. The sense of liberty loosed by Christ's lavish love flooded every fiber, core, and cranny of my being.

When I chose to *trust God*, I learned that Christ accepted, included, and loved me, right where I was, just as I was, *a tattered and shattered woman*. I encountered the reality of his love and knew without a doubt; he genuinely compassionately and sincerely cared for me. I discovered his passion was and is given regardless of my behaviors and regardless of my history. God loves me because he is God, and his love transcends any limited love I understand as a human being.

To me, God's love is as an ocean of endless waves rushing in unreserved depths in his forever pursuit and hold upon me. His love grasps me tightly, and he will never relinquish his caring grip on me or on you.

I believe and perceive that God holds this same genuine love for all humans, regardless of behavior. God's love is offered to all genders, races, socioeconomic classes, geographic regions, irrespective of wealth, or poverty. God grants love to everyone, no matter one's past! Everyone is included in his offering of love, even you.

God restores and reconciles relationships and community according to his purposed love. God's love reunites, converts, and forms according to his holy order and divine vision. This passion is the lens, the filter, and how I now view, see and understand a self, life, others, and God.

My Father's love is the origin of where I begin each day. His passion is my starting point and my position each morning. Divine love is where I live and where I draw from to receive fillings each moment, each hour, each day. His love overflows in his constant steady stream of abundant grace-life.

I am integrated, intertwined, tightly knitted, and intricately woven into the holy presence of this Triune Godhead. I am in union with the Father, Son, and Spirit, where I draw from the endless reservoir and bottomless well of love as my origin of whom I am.

Each day, you, me, and we together as God's family are knitted as One where we reside and dwell in this union as co-participators (*Ephesians 4:22–32*). In this communion, we are Christ's body expressive of the Father, who is truth, light, hope, and love.

11

Cultural Assimilation

> Stop imitating the ideals and opinions of the culture around you, but be inwardly transformed by the Holy Spirit through a total reformation of how you think.
>
> —Romans 12:2 (TPT)

> Through having different conversations, I have "real-eyesed" how common and easy it is to make decisions based on unquestioned belief systems, traditions and concepts we were raised with...by the very same humans who followed the exact same unquestioned patterns. These conditions govern our lives in *every* way imaginable.
>
> —Dana Gore

Children automatically, by nature, imitate the ideas and opinions of the culture and environment around them. A child's innocence is that they do not choose to do this, but it is a God-created natural-instinct.

As a child, harmed through years of abusive treatment, I had traits that manifested in distorted thought patterns as an adult driving my often out-of-control behaviors.

The Lord helped me to become aware of my need to have these traits transformed. One of the significant characteristics I had to deal with was the crippling fear that something terrible was about to happen. I walked around with this sense of gloom and doom just on the horizon and the feeling that danger could strike my loved ones at any moment.

These fears came from the fact that I had no sense of trusted safety nor did I feel protected. As a child, my home environment conditioned me to be fearful. This automatically played out as an adult, manifesting in high emotional states with anxiety and panic. The anticipated danger I felt in receiving the hateful messages from my dad's anger and rage became stuck energies in my nervous system.

My nervous system resulted in constant high-alert mode and agitated in heightened emotional fear feeling states. It was no wonder, as an adult, I was often over reactionary in vigorous explosive eruptions. As an adult, I naturally imitated the behaviors I saw exhibited in my home as a child. I had not learned how to develop any skills nor was I given any tools or role models to modify or regulate emotions.

This lack of bonded attachment to trust and safety caused an intense terror in me. As an adult, I subliminally thought, *If I don't control the people and situations around me to prevent them from being harmed, they too would be hurt.*

Thoughts such as these resulted in harboring pervasive inner guilt. I was unaware of this unconscious force driving me to be "overcontrolling" for decades. These drove my motivations, my daily intent, and pushed me to the brink of feeling insane.

How trauma impacted me regarding insecurities and not stopping the abuses forced me to feel a need to *control* everything, people and circumstances. To me, my loved ones were most at risk of falling prey to these unimaginable and invisible dangers that were a figment in my mind. As a child, I had no choice or ability to control anything happening to me or others in my home environment.

One of the dominant traits I struggled with for years was being super over-controlling and perfectionistic in my psyche. This urge to control hindered my closest relationships with my husband and children. Still, I had no idea how to stop this fanaticism.

I could not stop repetitive thought patterns such as "I have to be perfect or_____" (I will fail as a person). Fill in the blank with a word or words that define your feeling.

> Perfectionism is a self-destructive and addictive belief
> system that fuels this primary thought: If I look perfect,
> and do everything perfectly, I can avoid or minimize the
> painful feelings of shame, judgment, and blame.

> —Brene Brown

Perfectionistic tendencies are the consequences of unrealistic expectations placed on a child by parents. In my case, it was my dad's authoritarian rule and harsh religious traditions; there was nothing I did that could meet his standards.

In his view, I never measured up, even when doing what he asked to the best of my ability. It was never good enough. As a child, the unrealistic expectations gave rise to subliminal patterns driving me to be a *controlling perfectionist*. My core belief was I had to do everything correctly.

A lack of control in childhood manifests in adulthood to micro-manage these overwhelming fears by taking matters into one's hands (perfectionism, people-pleaser, overachieving). I felt an inner frenzy to protect my loved ones from these hidden and concocted fears, which only I noticed. Since I never developed an attachment or bond in feeling safe as a child, I assumed my loved ones were not safe. These anxious fears drove me to the point I tried to overprotect my loved ones from coming into any harm.

This unconscious element made me feel terrorized that something terrible was going to happen to my loved ones! This foreboding sense increased my anxiety to the point my nervous system went into a hypervigilant mode. This caused me to feel something terrible would happen to them. In my mind, this something terrible was right around the corner or could happen at any moment. This sense caused a horrid panic compelling me to the point of trying to control almost every little detail of their lives.

Little did I know what was happening was a natural means of reenacting my childhood fears in real life as an adult. I was unaware I was trying to go back into my child's self and protect the ones I was unable to when I witnessed abusive treatments to siblings and Mom.

These "*stuck*" nervous energies were playing a constant loop consuming my bodily system. These fears erupted frequently and seemingly out of nowhere. Sudden panic alerted me that this bad thing was about to happen if I did not remain vigilant to safeguard and protect my loved ones from these intangible harms.

When I began this inside-out journey, God enlightened me to what was occurring, and he gently held my heart, slowing, leading me out of this chaos and into the green pastures and fields of his safe harbor. In the green meadows and near the quiet pools of water, his deep, tender love nourished me with mercy and compassion.

Compassion asks us to go where it hurts, to enter into the places of pain, to share in brokenness, fear, confusion, and anguish. Compassion challenges us to cry out with those in misery, to mourn with those who are lonely, to weep with those in tears. Compassion requires us to be weak with the weak, vulnerable with the vulnerable, and powerless with the powerless. Compassion means full immersion in the condition of being human.

—Henri Nouwen

I chose as an act of my will to put faith in action. Taking small slow guarded steps in trusting my Father moved me into more than believing, in obtaining an ability to rely upon the unseen but the tangible presence of his love. This was discovering the source and the "thing" I had been searching for. This was the belonging I so desired: to be accepted, cherished, and truly loved. Life in Christ fulfilled and satisfied all I needed and wanted, bringing me home to myself.

The Father's passionate love for you, me, and us as his people is the authentic agent who leads each person into these same green pastures where identity, meaning, and life purpose are found in Christ and in Christ alone.

Love is our true destiny. We do not find the meaning of
life by ourselves alone—we find it with another.

—Thomas Merton

12

HABITS

In order to express what God's grace has done in us, we
have to form habits until all habits are merged in the perfect
relationship in love. God's commands are made to the life
of his Son in us, not to our human nature; consequently,
all that God tells us to do is always humanely difficult, but
it becomes divinely easy immediately we obey because our
obedience has behind it all the omnipotent grace of God.

—Oswald Chambers, *Grace & Truth: A Holy Pursuit*, pg. 77

To rebuild a life and maintain the sorts of change possible, I had
to do the mechanical part in developing healthier habits. To begin a
new routine usually means to stop some unhealthy obsession or pattern. The age-old myth that it takes twenty-one days to form a new
habit is not precisely correct.

A significant study was done on the length of time it takes to
develop a new pattern in the following research article, "How Are
Habits Formed? Modelling Habit Formation in the Real World," by
Phillippa Lally, Cornelia H. M. van Jaarsveld, Henry W. W. Potts,
and Jane Wardles int the *European Journal of Social Psychology*, published July 16, 2009 (https://doi.org/10.1002/ejsp.674).

The study above concluded it might take anywhere from two
months to 254 days for a new habit to become automatic. Although

many will place much attention on the result, what matters is that one begins to develop a new habit through regular repetition and practice.

When replacing unhealthy habits with healthier versions, the by-product is one's stress, anxiety, and depression levels begin to decrease. In developing practices or implementing some discipline related to the body or health, *setting goals, following through, and doing it become essential components of the process.*

A simple walking routine changed my life!

One of the first habits I started was walking. I tried to get daily exercise but had no craving to do hardcore exercises. So I chose to develop a walking routine, and in the beginning, it was for good reasons. But I discovered many more side benefits to walking that drew me into intimacy with God while also reducing anxiety and stress.

Walking as an exercise and as a disciple helped me establish a new routine and a new habit. This helped me in the beginning and maintaining other practices. When I wanted to start walking, I had to stop thinking about it, and I had to take action.

When we develop a regular practice that becomes a habit, it holds mechanical cues and rewards. Whenever the weather is permittable, my desire to step outside carried a signal or a "cue" when walking; I gained great enjoyment, pleasure, and fulfillment. I soaked in the views of picturesque flowers, plants, listened to the birds, and greeted strangers. I began to feel energized, motivated, and alive!

The phrase "Just do it" has become a mantra for me when wanting to start anything new or reinforce motivation to continue what I am doing presently. Instead of contemplating, ruminating, and over-thinking the thing, I begin by *just doing it!*

Suppose you have no physical limitations that prevent you from walking. In that case, this can be the most cost-effective and easy habit to begin to develop.

All that is required is a pair of supportive sneakers or walking shoes, and out the front door you go! I have found walking to be healthy, fun, and simple!

I walk different routes and often use this time to pray, sing, reflect, and talk with God. I find my mind relaxes in such an atmosphere, and I gain energy as my metabolism speeds up when I ramp up my steps.

The simple benefits I gain from walking are exercise, increasing metabolism, reduced stress, anxiety, increased motivation, and an enhanced pleasurable feeling. I know I am getting fresh air while helping to manage overwhelming emotions. These benefits offer internal and external rewards that motivate me to continue to practice walking as a healthy habit. When weather permits, the multiple benefits I gain outweigh the effort in just doing it by getting outside each day and walking.

I discovered a great deal of satisfaction and fulfillment in following through and successfully initiating and maintaining a walking routine. I have gained more rewards than I had first imagined!

Developing new habits requires *intentionality, self-discipline, hard work, commitment*, and *time*. What becomes important is not that you and I will make mistakes along the way. In this process, we continue moving forward, releasing "*stuck energies*."

Developing healthy patterns can take a long time. You and I must be willing to go through the uncomfortable emotions to obtain the fruit of our labor.

Old habits were formed by repetition and practice, so new habits are created through the same process, repetition, training, and discipline. Establishing new patterns and habits will lead us closer to God's intended purposes.

I became aware that I had to choose this new way. With God's help, you and I can succeed in developing healthier, more productive habits, and unique patterns in thinking and being.

You can progress in adding arm or leg weights, mixing up speed in intervals, and having a lot of fun along the way. This activity increases one's motivation. The reward itself is the feeling of satisfaction in completion, follow-through, and just doing it!

I recognized that acquiring new habits and developing changed patterns required new ways of thinking and gaining fresh perspectives. Learning to abide and respond as the new creation I am gifted in Christ became essential.

Developing new habits means that I am stopping old ones and replacing them with life-enhancing ones. If I were a couch potato and had very little motivation to walk, I would have to fight the urge to plop down on that couch and consume a bag full of chips. I would have to stop paying attention to the wanting to sit down and eat and focus on pushing myself out the door to walk.

In beginning any new routine, our thoughts, emotions, and body will resist.

I had to push against resistances in overcoming the inertia of doing nothing. In my quest to begin new thinking, new habits, and new practices, the mantra of "just doing it" became essential.

In establishing a walking practice, I had to set small obtainable and realistic goals. I began walking one block, then expanded this to two blocks, then three blocks, and gradually my walks became longer. Before I knew it, I was not even thinking of it as a chore but as an activity to enjoy.

I had to understand when I failed in my goal, like if I did not get out to walk a specific day, or perhaps several days, I had to learn to tell myself that it was okay.

I can pace, take breaks, and relax the demands I place on myself. I shifted my focus from not meeting every goal to appreciating the small accomplishments along the way.

My focus was redirected to the immediate and to what I could control, and I learned to let go of my perfectionistic demands I placed upon myself. I became inspired that developing new patterns and habits was more than possible with God's help.

My role was to apply the physical effort to do the mechanical part. God's purpose was to do the actual transformation needed in assisting me in the disciplines of retraining my mind in practices that fostered his image in mine.

Meditating on Scriptures and worshiping in song motivated me in this process. With God at the forefront of my thoughts, I moved forward to practicing new habits. Step by step, making manageable what was in my capacity to do and not sweating the small stuff if I did not accomplish every goal along the way.

You and I must keep in mind the transformation God desires is a process. The inside-out renewal process is a lifelong journey, not a final destination. We will continually be arriving but will never arrive at any pinnacle of perfection in this life. Each one of us is learning to make faith-choices in practicing to think according to God-directed strategies. Each one of us will make mistakes and err in judgment along the way. This is okay as it is part of the learning in Christ.

As believers, we are supplied with a *holy divine nature*, a *spirit-being* life, and a *magnificent, spectacular love* that surpasses human understanding in Christ.

Benefits to a walking routine

1. Walking (inside malls in cold weather or outside whenever possible):
   a. It provides exercise for the body, soul, and spirit.
   b. It offers alone time with God.
   a. Provides opportunity with those I meet

2. To share kindness, caring, and compassion.
3. To connect on an emotional level.
4. To share God's love.
5. Grants opportunity to worship while walking.
   a. Provides spiritual vigor and revitalization.
   b. Provides a connection with the Holy.
   c. Provides uplifting energies and rejuvenates.
   d. Provides attitude shift towards pleasant thoughts.
   e. Provides needed outlet from stress.
   f. Offers the opportunity to thank and praise God.
   g. Offers a shift in the attitude of gratefulness for life and God.

6. Praying while walking.
   a. Provides time for interceding.

b. Provides solitude time for reflection.
c. Gives sacred time to talk with God.
d. Provides renewal and reviving of prayer life.

Helpful tips in developing new habits

- Reflection, meditation, memorization of Scripture.
- Praising and thanking God with songs.
- Prayer—interceding for others.
- *Just do it!*
- Embrace the process—change takes hard work and time.
- It's okay to make mistakes.
- Hard work and effort build discipline.
- Consistency and persistence pay off.
- Determination to achieve one's goals invites God as a partner.
- Commit time daily to repetition and practice.
- Don't give up when weary or overwhelmed.
- Press into appropriating God's grace.
- Rest when needed; it's okay to take breaks and pace yourself.
- Let go of yesterday; view each day as a new beginning, a reset, a fresh start.
- Your starting place and position each day are in Christ.

Reflective encouragement

Take this example of beginning an exercise habit and apply these principles and methods shared in an area you want to see changed. Whether it is an exercise, an emotion (anger, rage, hate), a habit (smoking, drug, alcohol, overeating), a toxic relationship, or something else, choose one area to methodically and slowly work through. Beginning a walking routine helped me in the disciplined focus needed to develop other healthy habits while letting go and stopping the older ones that no longer supported. A simple walking routine riveted and energized me in ways I had never experienced. I felt envigored, motivated, and inertia dissipated and faded into the background.

Start with something you can accomplish and with something you have control in. When you gain a bit of success in the little steps forward and begin to feel a difference, this will motivate and encourage you to continue on this path. This transformation is more than possible as God works his holy love activity in and through you. Even though you may not feel or sense it at this time, you are personally known and deeply cherished, wanted, and loved by this same God. Father promised to reveal his love to anyone who asks. I pray he shows his love to you in profound ways and that you can know beyond a shadow of a doubt, his passion desires to abide in and with you, saturating and drenching every fiber of your being.

> Be faithful in small things because it is in
> them that your strength lies.
>
> —Mother Teresa

13

AN ATTITUDE OF GRATITUDE

For the word of God is alive and active. Sharper than any double-edged sword, it penetrates even to dividing soul and spirit, joints and marrow; it judges the thoughts and attitudes of the heart.

—Hebrews 4:12 (NIV)

How does one obtain an attitude of gratitude?

Gratitude is a trait that needs to be cultivated and nurtured. It is rarely mentioned or talked about in Christian circles. Yet, it is vital to develop attitude patterns according to Jesus's life. It is the person of Jesus who thinks, acts, and relates to the world through us as light, energy, and hope. A mindset of negativity and catastrophic thinking needs to be reformed according to Christ's life.

In my old self, I was programmed at dwelling on the negative and seeing the "bad" in things, people, and situations. I was an expert on viewing everything from this distorted perspective. Now God led me in this path, transforming my negative traits to obtain an *Attitude of Gratitude*.

It became necessary for me to incorporate several of the processes we have discussed in previous material in moving forward, learning to be thankful.

Healthy attitudes do not result from merely positive thinking or putting on some facade. Over the years, I met many "positive" persons whose tendency was to throw out clichés, quote Scriptures, and give platitudes to counteract the difficulties experienced in life.

Have you run into any of these people? I imagine you have, and most likely, it was not a pleasant experience. It is like having barbed-wire wrapped around your head and feeling as though someone is dragging you into some ditch, smothering you.

These types of "positive" persons fail to realize that even Jesus suffered and expressed himself through emotions. In my opinion, those who put on a façade of "positive thinking" often put on the fake pretense that "everything" is always pleasant, blissful, and excellent. They miss the boat on incorporating emotions as human beings into a vibrant faith.

Positivity, as a coping mechanism alone, is called denial. In fact, "positivity persons" struggle like crazy with all the emotions they pretend they don't have. They often fail to show empathy, compassion, understanding, and common sense in the face of adversity. These persons throw out platitudes, cliches, or quote Scriptures in their know-it-all approach to "fixing" another or pretending they have it altogether.

In life's reality, when we can accept dark emotions and difficult circumstances, we are expressing the Father in being human. We are incorporating an attitude of thanksgiving and appreciativeness, even from sorrowed suffering. Thankfulness and appreciativeness are traits that foster obtaining an attitude of gratitude.

Gratitude is a type of response that automatically wells up when someone does an unexpected act or gives us something not expected. This welling up also occurs when we give from our self unreservedly to others.

> Living gratefully begins with affirming the good and
> recognizing its sources. It is the understanding that life
> owes me nothing, and all the good I have is a gift.
>
> —Robert Emmons

When we allow the life of Christ to flow through us to others, we are exchanging an independent, self-centered life with "another being" way of living. This results in nurturing an attitude of gratitude.

Responding to others and relational difficulties in an attitude of appreciation and thankfulness fosters a deep sense of gratitude, regardless of their response. When we give, serve, help, or are outwardly focused toward other persons, we tend to soak in the well-being of thankfulness, appreciation, and gratitude.

Mindfulness practices cultivate traits such as thankfulness and appreciation. These practices ground you and me in responding to and from God's heart.

Integrating life challenges and one's emotional reactions is the continual process of how love transforms. This is how love moves us away from becoming stuck in unhealthy patterns, skewed attitudes, and self-centered obsessions.

In choosing intentionality as a lifestyle, Christ's love orientated me towards an attitude of thankfulness, where I learned to be appreciative, practicing simple gestures such as "Thank you," "You are welcome," "I appreciate you," and obtaining these traits. Daily writing or speaking the things I appreciated in my day or before retiring in the evening, viewing all that I admired and listing them, one by one, is a good practice. Thankful for essential things, like water, food, clothing, and housing. Enjoying the sun when it shines, the glorious colors in fall, the water gurgling in a creek, a baby's smile, a toddler's first steps, or those memories that warm you on the inside. All these practices help us in gaining gratitude.

I learned to appreciate the fact I can walk, cook, and care for myself and my family. I learned to look for God's goodness in others and the world. I learned to view God as a good kind Father who had plans to accomplish in and through me, beyond what I had imagined or believed possible.

It took time to slow down and walk as if my feet were kissing the ground. A meme, "Thich Nhat Han," a Buddhist monk, emphasized. Think of this meme next time you walk, and as you place your feet on the ground, visualize and imagine them kissing the ground. Feel the ground beneath your feet, sense its firmness, and in each step, breathe in the fresh air and fragrance of life. Take off your shoes and socks, stand on the ground outside or in the grass. Close your eyes and breathe in and out, standing there for several minutes. The tension your body holds can dissipate through this grounding technique as it discharges negative energies back into the ground.

In slowing down my mind when walking, I gazed more intently at clouds, trees, shrubs, flowers, plants, birds, and wildlife, breathing in *beauty, quiet, sacredness*. I soaked in sounds, smells, and sights. I took in long, slow, deliberate breaths of fresh air. I listened acutely and attentively where I often heard the Spirit speak in the wind, nature, and the wonder of God's designed creation. I stopped being in a hurry, ceased rushing through projects, slowed taking on missions, and quieted my mind in solitude activities.

Jesus was my reference point where I realized his life and his traits were already supplied to me. My need was to stop dwelling on my problems and issues and start looking outward toward his love and others outside my sphere.

Thankfulness is not putting on a plastic smile and pretending things are lovely when they were not. It does not deny when I feel miserable and afflicted. It is not about thinking that things are greener on the other side of my suffering and pain. Being thankful is not about dismissing, denying, or ignoring my present circumstances.

> It is always possible to be thankful for what is given
> rather than to complain about what is not given.
> One or the other becomes a habit of life.

—Elisabeth Elliot

Appreciation and thankfulness are about a person, and this person is Jesus Christ

I am grateful for the work Jesus finished on the cross. I am thankful for the Holy Spirit who empowers. I am appreciative of a love that transforms. I have reverence for the divine presence who lives, dwells, and takes up residence inside my human frame. I am grateful for my suffering and who I have become due to it. I am thankful to be alive and share in the hope of Christ as my source of living a meaningful and purposeful life, *even in the darkest of times.*

Jesus did not come to erase our difficulties. He offers you and me his presence in suffering and pain. Even Jesus suffered rejection and was a man who identified with sorrow and grief. Grief and sadness are heavy emotions that Jesus acutely bore as a man who was both divine and human.

> *He grew up before him like a tender shoot,*
> *and like a root out of dry ground.*
> *He had no beauty or majesty to attract us to him,*
> *nothing in his appearance that we should desire him.*
> *He was despised and rejected by mankind,*
> *a man of suffering, and familiar with pain.*
> *Like one from whom people hide their faces*
> *he was despised, and we held him in low esteem.*
> *Surely, he took up our pain*
> *and bore our suffering,*
> *yet we considered him punished by God,*
> *stricken by him, and afflicted.*
> *But he was pierced for our transgressions,*
> *he was crushed for our iniquities;*
> *the punishment that brought us peace was on him,*
> *and by his wounds we are healed.*
> *We all, like sheep, have gone astray,*
> *each of us has turned to our own way;*
> *and the LORD has laid on him*
> *the iniquity of us all.*
> *He was oppressed and afflicted,*
> *yet he did not open his mouth;*
> *he was led like a lamb to the slaughter,*
> *and as a sheep before its shearers is silent,*
> *so he did not open his mouth.*
> *By oppression and judgment, he was taken away.*
> *Yet who of his generation protested?*

For he was cut off from the land of the living;
for the transgression of my people he was punished.
He was assigned a grave with the wicked,
and with the rich in his death,
though he had done no violence,
nor was any deceit in his mouth.

—Isaiah 53:2–9 (NIV)

Practicing thankfulness rests on the assurance you and I have a person and a Lord named Jesus. He can appreciate and understand every emotion we experience. He was genuinely acquainted and profoundly moved by grief. He can empathize with each one of us in our misery, suffering, and pain. Jesus meets you and me right where we are and enters into all we experience physically, emotionally, mentally, and spiritually.

For one who has made thanksgiving the habit of
his life, the morning prayer will be, 'Lord, what
will you give me today to offer back to you?

—Elisabeth Elliot

We can be sure in his sovereign promise that his presence will be with us no matter the sorrow or difficulty we experience. Christ joins with us in every concern and issue. There is not one too small or too large for him to encompass. There is no amount of pain or loss we hold that Jesus is not familiar with having experienced. He is more than able to help you and me in this way.

Gratitude is strongly interconnected with an attitude in learning to appreciate the simple things in life. When we can learn to be thankful, acknowledge, accept, and allow all our emotional states (light and dark) as valid and valued, we will decrease our struggle.

Incorporating the processes above in moving forward, keep in mind that where you at right now does not determine the God-potential and the God-opportunities that lie on the road ahead. We can find our highest human purpose from suffering. It is often in pain and sorrows the most incredible opportunities present themselves. Contentment results when we let go of the struggle. Contentment occurs when we can appreciate what we suffered and grow in a courageous resilience from it. Incorporating and assimilating all we experience are necessary processes in discovering what it means to be a human being.

Our vision is so limited we can hardly imagine a love that does not show itself in protection from suffering... The love of God did not protect his own Son... He will not necessarily protect us—not from anything it takes to make us like his Son. A lot of hammering and chiseling and purifying by fire will have to go into the process.

—Elisabeth Elliot

The following excerpt is written by Dr. Paul T. P. Wong:

> According to this new science of resilience, the closest thing that feels like a positive state of mind in times of suffering is mature happiness (Wong & Bowers, 2018), characterized by calmness, contentment, inner harmony, and life satisfaction.
>
> This may be more important than fleeting feelings of excitement for long-term success. For example, Ali Pattilo (2020) reported that recent psychological research showed that "positive external outcomes cause only fleeting happiness. However, daily habits that cultivate positive thinking and optimism create sustainable happiness.

He pointed out that such actions as practicing gratitude, reviewing good memories, and activating your social network can increase mental health and improve performance. Similarly, Mayer Tamir, et al. (2017), found that happiness is more about having meaningful and valuable experiences than seeking pleasure and avoiding pain.

In a cross-cultural, multinational study, they found that participants who experienced more of the desired emotions, such as anger about abuse, reported greater life satisfaction and fewer depressive symptoms, even when those emotions were unpleasant.

"People want to feel very good all the time in Western cultures, especially in the United States," says Tamir, "Even if they feel good most of the time, they may still think that they should feel even better, which might make them less happy overall."

—*American Psychological Association*, 2017

The importance of this study is that happiness may involve some unpleasant emotions, resulting in ambivalence because of the coexistence of negative emotion with positive emotions. It takes practice to be able to hold two opposing feelings.

—According to Viktor Frankl and Dr. Paul T. P. Wong, *Made for Resilience & Happiness: Effective Coping with COVID-19*, pg. 42

To be grateful is to recognize the Love of God in everything he has given us—and he has given us everything. Every breath we draw is a gift of his love, every moment of existence is a grace, for it brings with it immense graces from him. Gratitude therefore takes nothing for granted, is never unresponsive, is constantly awakening to new wonder and to praise of the goodness of God. For the grateful person knows that God is good, not by hearsay but by experience. And that is what makes all the difference."

—Thomas Merton

Reflective encouragement

When you begin to be thankful, it might feel foreign or sur-real. You will not sense it as real in the beginning. Continue speaking the things you appreciate even if it feels uncomfortable as this is a normal part of this process. Eventually, your feelings will match your attitudes, and over time, you will sense more of an integration. Remember, it will be Christ in you, his thoughts, his motivation, his drive, and his love who forms an attitude of gratitude inside you as you press his sufficiency deeper, wider, and higher.

Join me in this prayer:

> My prayer is this: that he will lay out all the riches of his glory to give you strength and power, through his spirit, in your inner being; that the king may make his home in your hearts, through faith; that love may be your root, your firm foundation; and that you may be strong enough (with all God's holy ones) to grasp the breadth and length and height and depth, and to know the king's love—though actually it's so deep that nobody can really know it! So may God fill you with all his fullness.
>
> So to the one who is capable of doing far, far more than we can ask or imagine, granted the power which is working in us—to him be glory, in the church, and in King Jesus, to all generations, and to the ages of ages! Amen! (Ephesians 3:16–21 KNT)

14

MINDFULNESS

People who don't know God and the way he works fuss over
these things, but you know both God and how he works.
Steep your life in God-reality, God-initiative, God-provisions.
Don't worry about missing out. You'll find all your everyday
human concerns will be met. Give your entire attention to what
God is doing right now, and don't get worked up about what
may or may not happen tomorrow. God will help you deal
with whatever hard things come up when the time comes.

—Matthew 6:32–34 (MSG)

I lugged my dark past as a heavily weighted backpack into each
day, and I anxiously projected into a future not yet available. In the
above Scripture passage, Jesus was not saying to his disciples or to us
today that we cannot express worry or anxiety. Jesus emphasized not
to let those emotional tensions control or consume our thoughts and
manage the day.

I understood this teaching to mean my past is behind me and
my future is not yet. Recognizing all I have is right now. This present
moment to fully embrace life is applying the idea of Jesus's teaching
regarding mindfulness.

While it is difficult to eliminate the emotional responses to life,
it becomes necessary to redirect inordinate, focusing on either the

past or the future. Mindfulness does not deny the reality of our situations or emotional reactions. Jesus modeled a lifestyle that teaches how to regulate and manage these in healthy ways.

The biblical model of mindfulness helps establish order in retraining our thoughts. When we digest, ingest, and chew on the concepts and words written in the pages of the Bible, the Spirit secures fruitful thinking that fosters life. These spiritual truths anchor scattered thoughts and wild emotions, binding them to a sound foundation.

When we intentionally choose where and what to make a matter of our attention, God's love empowers us to create a lifestyle practicing mindfulness.

What is mindfulness? And how can this practice benefit me?

Mindfulness (some use the word *grounding*) *is characterized by meditation and relaxation techniques.*

Developing mindfulness practices is to help us become more aware, but not in a self-conscious manner. Mindfulness requires an opening and receptivity to explore the inner chasms of our being. It requires an interest in discovering the interior domain. As a believer, mindfulness includes God as an intimate partner in these practices.

Practicing mindfulness is often used to help persons reduce stress and rewire the brain after trauma, retraining the mind to build new neuropathways. Mindfulness practices can free us from the grip of self-judgment, shame, and inadequacy. These practices can open our hearts in receptivity to a deeper level of experiencing God's love and compassion. Receiving and accepting God's love is vitally necessary to love a self and others.

In Philippians 4:12–13, Paul emphasizes a mindful attitude of contentment is a necessary trait of a disciple:

> I know how to do without, and I know how
> to cope with plenty. In every possible situation,
> I've learned the hidden secret of being full and
> hungry, of having plenty and going without. It's

this: I have strength for everything in the one
who gives me power.

Paul emphasizes an attitude of thankfulness, regardless of life
events and circumstances. When we acknowledge, accept, and allow
where we are presently (emotions and circumstances) and then live
in Christ, our soul is delighted. We are less likely to succumb to fret-
ting, worrying, tossing, and turning it all in our heads. We are more
likely to recognize where we are and let go of what we have no control over. The anxiety, worry, and fears result from not being able to
control, fix, or remedy the "thing'" you obsess about day and night.

As Christians, we recognize emotions, and we consider the reality of our circumstances. Still, we can learn to let go of the negativity associated with specific emotions. We can choose to think about
different things, which requires continually responding to Christ's
spirit. We can choose to let go of the baggage we carry in those heavily weighted backpacks—*anger, unforgiveness, hurts.*

We can simply say, "No, I am not going to think about that
now, but instead, I will choose to believe this verse in Philippians.
I will consider using scriptures to replace tendencies to engage in
obsessive thinking about the future or the past."

It is essential to discover what we are making a matter of our
review. We must understand how we interpret those thoughts; a lot of
our suffering results from how we wrongly interpret/label thoughts,
emotions, events, and relationships.

If we label thoughts as evil, horrible, and impossible constructs
to overcome, we will be limited in moving forward.

A biblical model to developing a mindfulness practice

We can select a biblical model of creating mindfulness practices
in Christ. His life fosters new life when we abandon negative and
self-defeating thinking.

We can choose to surrender the tendency to fret about things
that have not yet happened or obsess about the past. We can choose

to be intentional and redirect our thoughts onto other things that strengthen, empower, and cultivate Christ's life.

Jesus taught his followers the importance of what and where they placed their attention was an essential component to fully embrace living in the moment.

Jesus addresses you and me in this same manner today

Jesus placed a great deal of emphasis on *living in the now* and *living simply*. The practice of mindfulness incorporates meditation and relaxation techniques that help individuals become aware of inner turbulence and instruct how to calm them. Mindfulness practices help develop an internal awareness of the spiritual, of the real you, of negativity, etc.

One learns to pay attention to the internal realm of thoughts, feelings, and sensations. The goal of doing this is to stop labeling and categorizing emotions as bad, wrong, or right. The objective is to adopt a neutral stance regarding feeling states and moods.

In the East, mindfulness is a practice used by Buddhists. In Buddhist philosophy, they see that suffering results from undue attachments to this world. They attempt to detach themselves from thought patterns and emotions that entangle them. This is their path out of pain and suffering. This practice is what they believe will lead them into a state of nirvana or bliss. The way they practice mindfulness is very much a self-conscious activity, negating any participation with God.

They try to obtain a nonjudgmental view of thoughts, allowing them to come and go, not labeling or becoming stuck in them. This concept is part of their spiritual journey and is a central theme of their religion. Mindfulness practices originated from the East, and Christians fear anything they view as Eastern mysticism. They fear this could open them to "evil" or dark influences. They fear these practices are not from God.

Yet, when bringing up the word mindfulness, many Christians fear emptying their minds leads to demonic influences. They also mistakenly view meditation as encouraging denial of reality and promotes an unhealthy degree of self-focus.

These concerns are valid if one's practice of mindfulness stems from a secular mindset. In the East, mindfulness presents a one-way relationship. What Eastern thought promotes is that you pay attention only to yourself. That approach is contrary to scriptural teaching.

Although both philosophies are spiritual practices, the Judeo-Christian belief includes God as a person and a living being who is an active agent in their lives. Christians can and do adopt mindfulness practices in allowing God to be an intricate and dynamic participant.

While mindfulness is a therapeutic technique in psychology and a significant Buddhist philosophy, most in these fields leave out God's person as a divine source to invite into this practice.

The biblical view is we have the mind of Christ and evaluate everything in light of having an integrated and interconnected relationship with the person of God. The thoughts we think align with the life of Christ in us, and we respond according to his nature.

As believers, we can incorporate mindfulness practices in a Christ-integrated way as useful methods to enhance our physical, mental, and spiritual health, fostering well-*being*.

Mindfulness can be compatible with a biblical worldview *when it is rooted in Scripture and focuses on one's relationship with God.*

The biblical model of mindfulness has a lot to say about keeping our thoughts focused on God's truth.

- I meditate on all your works and consider what your hands have done (Psalm 143:5 NIV).
- I will consider all your works and meditate on all your mighty deeds (Psalm 77:11–12 NIV).
- Think about things above, not the things that belong on the earth (Colossians 3:3 KNT).
- "[B]ut people whose lives are determined by the spirit, focus their minds on matters to do with the heart of Father (Romans 8:5 KNT).
- Pray on every occasion in the spirit, with every type of prayer and intercession (Ephesians 6:18 KNT)!

- May the words of my mouth and the meditation of my heart be pleasing in your sight LORD, my Rock, and my Redeemer (Psalm 19:14 NIV).
- This is how you should think among yourself—with the mind that you have because you belong to the Messiah, Jesus (Philippians 2:5).
- Meditation appears in the Bible as a practice to implement (Psalm 63:6).
- Redirecting thoughts towards the good and the truth (Philippians 4:8).
- Worrying into a future not yet here distracts us from living in the moment (Matthew 6:25–34).
- The transformation from old patterns to godly patterns occurs through renewing our minds (Romans 12:2).

Those who practice mindfulness will see significant gains in emotional regulation. When these practices are adopted into one's daily lifestyle, mindfulness can help almost every psychological condition and is often useful in conjunction with therapy.

Mindfulness helps in the following ways: reduces stress, lessens pain, relieves anxiety, unifies relationships, builds inner awareness, solidifies good attention, disciplines thoughts, fosters an attitude of gratitude, cultivates accurate perceptions, awakens alertness, and nourishes sensitivity to the Spirit.

Walk as if you are kissing the Earth with your feet.

—Thich Nhat Hanh, *Peace Is Every Step: The Path of Mindfulness in Everyday Life*

Establishing a mindfulness practice

1. I am paying (not obsessing over) attention to thoughts, feelings, and sensations at the moment (review chapter titled "A God-Directed Strategy").

2. The idea is not to think of thoughts or emotions as good or bad. We are trying to distance ourselves from judging or labeling. We simply want to notice as a neutral observer what is happening inside. We want to put away our tendency to categorize emotions as right or wrong.

3. We want to invite emotions as allies, *acknowledging, accepting, and allowing them expression.*

4. We welcome all our emotions as intimate companions.

5. Be willing to let go of labeling emotions. It is when we hold onto anxiety, worry, and fear we become stuck in them. We associate negative feelings with a poor self-concept and then view ourselves from a negative filter.

6. The idea is not to eradicate emotions but rather to *reduce inordinate attention or focus* on them. We don't want to become cyclically stuck in them or let them rule or control us.

7. Jesus fully expressed emotions. Although some in Christian circles put their feelings and common sense on a shelf, Jesus never did that.

8. Jesus lived life fully expressive of all the emotions common to humans. He relates and identifies deeply with all we experience.

9. We are fully expressive and created humans as God's love expresses all facets of human beings.

10. Disentangling ourselves from inordinate focus provides consistency in moving forward.

11. Recognizing God is good all the time. Integrating light and dark emotions as expressions become necessary.

12. We are the expression of God in all our emotions, light, and dark.

Reflective encouragement

Self-criticism, insecurity, and shame can be destructive to a relationship with God, self, and others. Suppose we allow these emotions and beliefs to fester. In that case, these feelings can feed into lifelong patterns that negatively impact how we view God, self, others, and the world. When caught in this unhealthy cycle, persons can develop debilitating brain patterns that preserve their feelings of inadequacy and harm their mental health.

The thoughts we think directly impact our physical, mental, and spiritual well-being. Distorted, skewed, and false patterns lead to shutting down, distancing from others, and result in an inability to experience the openness, warmth, and support of a healthy restored relationship with God, self, and others.

The good news is *research has shown that fifteen minutes of mindfulness* practice daily can change the brain's structure, enabling us to build healthy new patterns that result in healthier functioning as a whole. This daily routine can create new ways of thinking that lead to meaningful connections while cultivating an openness to trust and love.

Incorporating healthy practices into our day and inviting the Holy Spirit as an intimate partner can free us from the clutches of self-judgment, shame, and inadequacy. Our hearts can be inspired towards a more in-depth experience and bonded connectivity in God's love.

We can practice mindfulness while cooking, eating, walking, listening to music, relaxing. We can choose to slow down thoughts when cooking and enter into the moment, intentional about what we are doing. We see the food, smelling the food, appreciating the colors, breathing in and out. We caringly place the meal decoratively on our plate, pacing our activity, engaging our senses, and living in the smells, sights, and sounds.

Mindfulness programs have been implemented and utilized across disciplines and used in almost every area and field: religion, education, corporate workplaces, prison/jail, mental health, rehabilitation centers, hospitals, wellness centers, trauma clinics, etc. We can thoughtfully and prayerfully consider using these practices to supplement any therapeutic interventions. If you are in therapy, ask your therapist to guide you in applying mindfulness practices to a daily regimen. If you are not presently in treatment, ask a coach or sign up for an online forum. Many videos on YouTube will guide you through meditation with music, sounds, and scenery.

Scientific research has shown that mindfulness can reduce bothersome symptoms such as pain, stress, anxiety, and depression. Daily practice can help individuals and communities effectively manage life challenges in maintaining health and wellness living to their best potential as a human being.

Although mindfulness is a controversial topic in Christian circles, we don't have to fear using these techniques if we include God in our practice. In developing new habits, we want to incorporate the practice of mindfulness. As we practice each day, we may notice our perspective slowly shifts from inordinate attention to the negative. Our view is reoriented according to the spirit in Christ. Christ in us moves us into the realm of possibilities that occur as his mind and his thoughts renew ours.

It is known that even when the most stressed brain is
allowed to unwind, much past suffering can be erased
and new brain circuits encouraged to grow.

—Tim Gallwey, *The Inner Game of Stress*
(2010), www.theinnergame.com

EPILOGUE

In reviewing the past, although I walked for many years in the *dark valley of suffering, I saw signs that my Lord Jesus had walked with me.* He deposited those sensations of safety, innocence, and peace from the time spent at "The Farm" as signs of his presence. He placed those treasured memories inside me as reminders of his care. He embedded truths of connected bonding I felt with family and nature while roaming those lands in the rolling hills of Pennsylvania. God shepherded me as a child, and he shepherded me in the years of suffering as an adult and he is shepherding me now.

Jesus is our Good shepherd, *even when we don't understand.*

There are seasons in our lives we will not sense or feel God's presence, *but do not mistake those times for his absence.*

I am now confident he never left me alone in my pained childhood. I am sure he never relinquished his desired and personal love for me, *even when I rejected him.* I am secure that God's love is faithful in that he provided a means when I did not see the path forward.

I am gently reminded that my story is not one of healing myself. I am not who I am now by my strength, education, profession, strategizing, or human ingenuity. I am not liberated from the bondage of the past today due to my spiritual resume, accolades, or what I did or did not do. I am freed from the oppression of trauma today due to God's loving mercy, period. This freedom does not mean I no longer suffer or experience difficulties. This freedom releases the holds they once had on me and grants a hope in the midst of suffering.

My story, your story, and the story God is writing for all humanity are incorporated into God's larger narrative. The Word of God tells of a Lord whose revealing and redemptive purposes are found in a spirit-being who created each human from desired love—

to love and be loved. We were created with a God-dimension inside to belong intimately in the bondedness of his love. Each human was perfectly and uniquely designed to be completed in the inclusiveness of this radical infinite and perpetual life fostering love *where nothing else compares.*

When we try to replace this God-love dimension with anything else, we will wander restlessly searching and experimenting, trying to fill this emptiness or "void" with things offered in this world.

In my childhood, I often talked to a God who always felt distantly removed. I failed to *"see"* his activity and care in my life. I focused on the darkness, the pain, and anger. I missed the ray of hope and the light of his love he was shining inside the cracks and in the shattering.

Without a doubt, it is evident to me that over those many years, he supplied glimpses and emblems of his care and love to me *that I denied.*

One of the many ways I sensed God's love was in the known peace and tranquility I sensed in the marvel of nature. Another way he showed his care was in the language of his love and marks of his presence that deeply touched me when raising my children. One of the most significant signs in his presence was a felt belonging to his love when worshiping, *cocooned in his warmth.*

The most visible sign of God's love to me was found in my husband's trusted loyalty, whose faithfulness was a steady rock in my turmoil. My husband's compassion, wisdom, and faith all helped me become who I am today. He challenged me when I did not want to listen. He spoke truth into the lies I was believing. He confronted the false ideas I had.

God had provided and is still providing me with a man who is my wise counsel and a human in the flesh who I can always count on for constancy.

Through my husband's genuineness, I learned to trust and know the revelation of the Father's love for me as a woman.

Sometimes we all need hearts in the flesh to remind and show us God is with us, and he does care *all the time!* God's provision is seen when he brings angels with skin on them, other persons to support, encourage, and help us. Our role is to be spiritually attuned, listening attentively to his Spirit, *remaining receptive to his love.*

God revealed his love through my husband, my children, friends, and the world around me, *even when I failed to recognize him.* He announced his passion from the images, sensations, sights, smells, and remnants of my great-grandmother's simple uncluttered faith in the solitude comforted solace.

I carried the quiet confident trust of a deep faith God deposited from those times visiting "The Farm" as a sanctity in my mind, body, and spirit. I carried the sense of his still small voice from those meadowlands and forested woods as tightly interwoven remnants of his tender shepherding love.

Perhaps we will discover living out our faith is not about achieving, arriving, perfecting, or developing anything.

Maybe faith in Christ is more about being relationally intertwined into the center of the Father's heart, immersed and enveloped in an endless, expansive never-ending and perpetual life gifting love.

Maybe God only desires me, you, and us as a community to be just where we are and just who we are in all our human weaknesses and uncertainties. Maybe in the unknowns and in the complicated troubles of our day, God reveals his most remarkable treasure to all mankind; *that he remains faithful to love each one, all the time!*

Could my great-grandmother's simple, uncluttered faith be the love God wants to reveal in the sensations, images, and in the people all around us that we are missing?

Are the remnants hidden in our hearts of seasons of innocence, stillness, peace, and contentment be the holy presence that our Lord desires to make known to us today?

Is God revealing his ravishing spectacular love to me and you and us as a community in the ordinariness of our everyday being?

Could the symbols I remember and the volumes they spoke about God's love I viewed when visiting the "*Farm*" of great-grandma's tiny bedroom, the Bible, twin bed, and rosary beads be signs that God is in it all, *even when nothing makes sense?*

Perhaps this faith is all about responding to the Spirit in the small "stuff." Maybe *expressing the Father's heart* is seen in the tasks of each day and the kind gestures we extend to people we meet along the way.

Perhaps faith lived practically is displayed in the way we care for others, how we offer help, and the way we take notice when one is in need. Perhaps expressed faith is a behind the scenes kind of thing, a lifestyle in being for the *"other" that is hidden in Christ.*

Maybe the suffering we experience now and the difficulties we will participate in the future are drawing us ever nearer to the Father's heart. Perhaps in these unexpected challenges and in the pained sorrow of living, the Father is unveiling our highest *need to come to him repeatedly and repeatedly* to receive mercy and grace.

Maybe when we continually receive his constant offer of love, responding from Christ as our no lack-supplier of immeasurable grace, he unwraps and unfolds what it truly means to be an authentic and real *human being.*

I am convinced God led me through the valley of the shadow of death, living in the destabilizing aftermath of trauma, so I would come to the place of trusting in him alone as *source and sufficiency of all life.*

References

Hall, Julie H. and Frank D. Fincham. "Self-forgiveness: The step-child of forgiveness research." *Journal of Social and Clinical Psychology*, 24, (2005): 621-637.

Hillenbrand, Laura. *Unbroken: A World War II Story of Survival, Resilience, and Redemption*. Random House, 2014.

Krause, Neal and Christopher G. Ellison. "Forgiveness by God, Forgiveness of Others, and Psychological Well-Being in Late Life." *Journal for the scientific study of religion*, 42, No. 1, (2003): 94.

Larkin, Heather, Vincent J. Felitti and Robert F. Anda. "Social Work and Adverse Childhood Experiences Research: Implications for Practice and Health Policy." *Social Work in Public Health*, 29, No. 1, (2014): 1-16.

Larkin, Heather, Joseph J. Shields and Robert F. Anda. "The Health and Social Consequences of Adverse Childhood Experiences (ACE) Across the Lifespan: An Introduction to Prevention and Intervention in the Community." *Journal of Prevention & Intervention in the Community*, 40, No. 4, (2012): 263-270.

Lorenc, Theo, Ssrah Lester, Katy Sutcliffe, Claire Stansfield and James Thomas. "Interventions to support people exposed to adverse childhood experiences: systematic review of systematic reviews." *BMC Public Health*, 20, (2020): 657.

McConnell, John M. and David N. Dixon. "Perceived forgiveness from God and self-forgiveness." *Journal of Psychology and Christianity*, 31, (2012): 31-39.

Ross, Colin A. "Talking about God with Trauma Survivors." *American Journal of Psychotherapy*, 70, No. 4 (2016): 429-437.

Walker, Donald F., Henri W. Reid, Tiffany O'Neill and Lindsay Brown. "Changes in Personal Religion/Spirituality During and

After Childhood Abuse: A Review and Synthesis." *Psychological Trauma Theory Research Practice and Policy*, 1, No. 2 (2009): 130-145.

Wong, Paul T. P. The positive psychology of grit: The defiant power of the human spirit. [Review of the movie Unbroken, 2014]. *PsycCRITIQUES,* 60, No. 25 (2015).

Wong, Paul T. P. "Self-Transcendence: A Paradoxical Way to Become Your Best." *International Journal Of Existential Positive Psychology*, 6, No. 1 (2016): 9.

Wong, Paul T. P. *Made for Resilience and Happiness: Effective Coping with COVID-19 According to Viktor E. Frankl and Paul T. P. Wong.* Toronto, ON: INPM Press, 2020a.

Wong, Paul T. P. Existential Positive Psychology and Integrative Meaning Therapy. *International Review of Psychiatry,* (2020b).

Zarse, Emily M., Mallory R. Neff, Rachel Yoder, Leslie Hulvershorn, Joanna Chambers and Robert A. Chambers. "The adverse childhood experiences questionnaire: Two decades of research on childhood trauma as a primary cause of adult mental illness, addiction, and medical diseases." *Cogent Medicine* 6, No. 1 (2019).

Practices and Exercises

If we keep practicing, what we practice becomes our second
nature, then in a crisis and in the details of life we shall find that
not only will the grace of God stand by us, but also our own
nature. Whereas if we refuse to practice, it is not God's grace
but our own nature that fails when the crisis comes, because we
have not been practicing in actual life. We may ask God to help
us but he cannot, unless we have made our nature our ally.

—Oswald Chambers, *Grace & Truth: A Holy Pursuit*, pg. 17

When developing new practices, keep in mind that you will
not sense any changes or differences quickly. Yet, over time and the
more you spend a committed time, practicing a bit each day, you
will notice a profound difference in how you think and feel. Change
takes time and patience.

Overachievers will need to back down on moving forward too
fast or trying to accomplish too much too soon. Those who have
stuffed feelings and are "numb" will want to get in touch with these
dormant emotions that need expression. Pacing, taking breaks, resting, and balancing work with pleasure is vital to keep in mind.

Select one of the following methods to begin practicing. If what
you pick does not work for you, no problem, move onto another
technique. Not all of these exercises will work for everyone as each
person is uniquely created.

I encourage you to give the method you select at least thirty
days before moving on to explore a different one. Like the chapter
on habits affirm, it may take almost a year to develop a steady new
discipline or practice. Try not to focus on results as this is a jour-

ney and not a final point to arrive at some perfection or pinnacle of achievement.

Remember, there is no rush or hurry, and pacing your activity will require discipline, regularity, and dedication on your part.

God never hurries. There are no deadlines against which he must work. Only to know this is to quiet our spirits and relax our nerves.

—A. W. Tozer, *The Pursuit of God*

Retraining Thoughts (A)

Working through unhealthy thought patterns

What we think directly impact the way we feel. Our thoughts take root and determine behavior. Our behaviors can become unmanageable unless we learn to address faulty thinking patterns.

We experience an event or a conversation or some interaction (the stimulus). We have beliefs about that, and we interpret meaning from these encounters. We may assume wrongly or interpret these from a negative filter or skewed mindset. If we have twisted belief systems, these will impact what we receive as messages. We will then internalize inaccurate truths, which we then project onto others or a self.

How we interpret an event/interaction results in feelings and emotional reactions. It takes repetition and regularity for us to unlearn false beliefs and to retrain our minds in new ways, but this is more than possible. It just takes willingness, dedication, time, and trusting God.

Our behavior is acted out due internalization of assumptions or labeling that is not accurate. These distorted judgments we conclude is how we label the event/interaction with thoughts/feelings. Then these conclusions become displaced in our psyche as "truths," even when not true.

You might want to get a notebook to use for the practices.

Evaluating thoughts with evidence

1. When thinking about specific thoughts, we can begin to evaluate if our thoughts are beneficial. We can review a thought to see if it is helpful. If it is not helpful, we want to know that.
2. Sometimes we all have dysfunctional thought patterns. Often, we think thoughts that aren't entirely true.
3. Some thought patterns become an all or nothing ("If one person says something negative about me, that means everyone thinks the same thing about me"). Generalizing what one person says and placing that onto everyone else putting them into the same category is not a realistic nor is this a healthy coping method.
4. Some thought patterns are focused on the worst possible outcome ("If I try to get better, things will only get worse").
5. Some people become stuck in negative thinking ("Nothing ever works out for me" or "I'll never feel okay again").
6. We want to find evidence if what we think is right or is it inaccurate:
7. (a) proof that the thought might not be true; (b) evidence that the idea is true; (c) evidence that the thought is harmful. (d) evidence if the thought is beneficial.
8. When we are feeling emotions such as fearful, sad, angry, worried, anxious, we can take them one at a time and ask ourself:
9. (a) What thoughts are going through my head? (b) What am I saying to myself? (c) How does this make me feel?
10. Thinking a thought does not mean the idea is the real truth. It also means you don't have to keep thinking that way. You can choose what to think about and you can choose to think on different things.
11. In each thought, examine the evidence to see if (a) the idea is real; (b) if the idea is helpful; (c) if the thought is not helpful.

In your journal, list a few thoughts you had today. I will list a few examples to help you get started. You may be saying the following to yourself: "*This is too hard. I can't do this. This work makes me angry. I feel like giving up.*"

Take each idea separately.

Ask yourself the following questions. Is this idea true? Is this idea helping me? Is this idea false? Is this idea hurting me?

Then ask the following two questions.

1. What did I discover?
2. Does the evidence show the thought might not be accurate?
3. Did the evidence show the thought might not be helpful?
4. If so, then think to yourself, *What could I replace the thought/ idea with that will be more accurate?*
5. What can I replace the thought with that will be more benefit to my whole person?

You are in control of your thoughts. You can choose to replace an inaccurate thought (assumption/belief) with accurate ones that produce confident strength.

This process will require regularity, practice, practice, and practice.

Repeat your mantra to yourself; *there is no hurry and there is no rush.*

There is no place to arrive.

I am okay.

Review the following ideas:

Thought: *If one person says something negative about me, that means everyone thinks the same thing about me.* Generalizing an entire group of persons based on what one or two may say does not mean it is true.

Thought: *I cannot do this work, it is just impossible!* How do you know you cannot do this work? Have you given it 100 percent?

When doing this work, remember to invite the Holy Spirit in the process. Review the chapter on "A God-Directed Strategy to stop overthinking, ruminating and obsessing.

Our thoughts and how they relate to the trauma(s) affect how we feel and act. The thoughts and how they are interpreted impact other areas of our life. Ideas can help us feel better or they can keep us feeling upset.

Investigating and identifying some of your thoughts related to the trauma(s) become necessary to sort out the underlying emotions and outward behaviors. We can assess our ideas to see if they are untrue and/or unhelpful (by examining the evidence). If the thought or belief is not helpful or untrue, you can then explore alternative views and replace the thought with a more accurate and/or more helpful thought/idea/concept.

Replacing some of these untrue or exaggerated thoughts with scriptural truths can be an affirming way to address faulty beliefs.

Exercise on Listening (B)

Listening

It can be tough to even believe that God is listening. It can be scary to trust he is right here with you; even though you may believe it, you don't feel it. This is the struggle. All we can do is continue putting one foot in front of the other, trusting God is with you all the time. Trust in the emotions. Trust in the fear. Trust in the process.

It takes trust on so many levels. Trust is not something we know from having suffered from child abuse. No one listened to us as a child. This caused increasing fears that seemed as impenetrable as the invisible steel caged walls we built to defend ourselves from any future hurts.

But God makes a way when we see no way. His love unlocks barriers and they begin to crumble. His love dismantles fear.

Trust results when we *discern* God's voice among the chatter in our heads. We realize it is okay to trust his love to let go of fears. We realize it is okay to trust his love to release tension and anxiety. We discover it is okay to trust his love to find rested sanctity.

Overcoming the mindset that God is not listening, and he does not care can be one of the most challenging battles we can face. This type of overcoming results when love is received. Love dismantles the fear God is not listening. Love removes the barriers and restores safety and trust.

For this to occur, we need to be willing participants. All that is required to begin our role in moving beyond the past is willingness. When we remain receptive to God, he is faithful to do the work he promised. Receptivity requires listening.

This does and will take time. Give yourself permission to take whatever time is needed. There is no rush; there is no hurry. This is a journey and not some pinnacle of achieving. Try and welcome the frustration in quieting the inner chaos. Recognize this is a long-term process in learning to listen.

Be mindful that God is the love transforming as you apply the mechanical effort.

Listening is one of the first traits we need to develop and one I would like to emphasize. Here are a few listening thoughts to consider:

1. Listening takes trust. Trust is what we lack. Trust was shattered from abuse. Our lack of listening has huge negative ramifications. Trust is an act of faith. It takes trust on so many levels, and trust is what we lack.
2. Listening restores trust.
3. Listening to the love in you. Listening to love restores and heals wounds.
4. Listen deeply to love as light and mercy.
5. Listen quietly.
6. Listening is a choice.
7. Listen intently.
8. Listen in wanting to hear.
9. Listen openly to discover.
10. Listen to the spirit's silence.

11. Listen to the beat of your heart.
12. Listen to the wind.
13. Listen to the birds.
14. Listen attentively.
15. Listen with no agenda. Let go of the critical voice. Let go of the judging voice.
16. Listen as an act of the will. Choose to stop talking, rambling, obsessing. Choose listening.
17. Listen actively.
18. Listen authentically. Sincerity restores trust. Genuineness awakens trust.
19. Listen to surrender.
20. Listen eagerly.
21. Listen longingly.

Here are a few more mantras for you to repeat to yourself. You can be your own coach. You can help yourself by affirming you are human and all humans have limitations.

It is okay to be right where I am.
It is okay to make mistakes.
It is okay to feel whatever I am experiencing.
I am doing the best I can in this moment.
Opportunity and possibilities are ahead of me.
All I have to do is continue putting one foot in front of the other.
I acknowledge, welcome, and accept the process and all that comes with it.

Practical application

I will share an insightful method of how to incorporate listening in real-life applications. Listening is necessary for us to learn to stop reacting and train ourselves to respond to another in the right manner and with an even tone. I am involved with an organization out of Canada called the International Network on Personal Meaning of whom Dr. Paul T. P. Wong is the founder and president. The following is an excerpt copied exactly as written from material written by Dr. Wong:

> Based on Frankl's writings and the following famous quote typically attributed to Frankl, I believe, can be best understood as a 3-second pause that can save us from many problems. These 3 seconds will create enough space for us to make the right decision, which may mean a different outcome, a different destiny: "*Between stimulus and response, there is space. In that space is our power to choose our response. In response lies our growth and freedom.*" (Viktor E. Frankl)

1. The 1st second. What is happening in this situation (Mindfulness)? We need to observe what is unfolding with *mindfulness* or *self-detachment* in Frankl's terminology. This brief intentional pause can make all the difference because it enables us to suspend our impulse, bias, or emotional reaction in a split second to allow for more accurate stress appraisal (Peacock & Wong, 1990). Don't panic even when you feel overwhelmed by all the dark forces attacking you. One moment of stillness can save your life and turn the tide in your favor. One moment of pause will give you the necessary time to seek guidance from your soul and/or from a higher power for the right response.

2. The 2nd second. What are my options, or what kind of freedom do I have in this situation (Reflection on liberty)? Whatever the circumstances, we always have some degree of autonomy or control; even in the worst-case scenario of having a gun pointed at our head

to obey an evil order, we still have the freedom of attitude to take a stance. It is always possible to maintain the space to protect our inherent human dignity and core value by boldly declaring: "You can destroy my body, but you cannot kill my soul." We have the freedom to choose to die happily as a martyr, whereby we instantly transform the human tragedy into a heroic triumph.

3. The 3rd second. What is the right thing to do? How can I make a congruent decision with my life purpose and core value (Frankl, 1988)? We are constantly confronted with the existential dilemma of choosing between expediency and meaning. Deciding to gain some practical advantage, we may have to sacrifice our integrity or sell our soul, but choosing to do the right thing, we may have to face persecution and suffering.

These 3 seconds may even buy you enough time to laugh at the absurdity of life and make yourself happy: "Humour…can afford an aloofness and an ability to rise above any situation, even if only for a few seconds." (Frankl, 1985, p. 63)

—According to Viktor E. Frankl and Paul T. P. Wong, *Made for Resilience and Happiness: Effective Coping with COVID-19*

Mindfulness Exercise (C)

Mindfulness means maintaining a moment-by-moment awareness of our thoughts, feelings, bodily sensations, and surrounding environment, through a gentle, nurturing lens. Mindfulness also involves acceptance, meaning that we pay attention to our thoughts and feelings without judging them—without believing, for instance, that there's a "right" or "wrong" way to think or feel in a given moment. When we practice mindfulness, our thoughts tune into what we're sensing in the present moment rather than rehashing the past or imagining the future.

Mindfulness can turn your fear into calmness and sadness into joy. But it does not come easy; you need to practice the following spiritual skills, represented by the acronym OCEAN:

Open-mindedness. Focus on the present with an open mind. Pay attention to the present moment as life unfolds. Pay attention to what you see, hear, smell, taste, and touch right now.

Describe what the water tastes like when you drink it or what you see when you regard the person who stands before you. Your ability to focus determines what you will find. Openness means the absence of biases and prejudice.

Compassion. See others as people like you. We are all struggling with our problems. We are all on the same train, heading to the same destination—death. When you see others as members of the same family coping with the stress of life, your heart will sense compassion.

Empathy. People are complicated and difficult to understand. When you feel annoyed with someone, remember that they may have their reasons for behaving that way. Others may feel the same way about you because they don't understand your intention and reason. Empathy simply means I try to understand you by trying to be in your shoes.

Acceptance. Accept life as it is. Accept others as they are. Accept yourself, warts and all.

Non-judgement. Take a deep breath and see what is going on without judgement. You can do that only by "self-detachment" or "self-distancing," according to Frankl. Look at each person with a fresh pair of eyes, without all the past baggage of painful memories, problem-saturated stories, and intense emotions of love or hate.

—According to Viktor E. Frankl and Paul T. P. Wong, *Made for Resilience and Happiness: Effective Coping with COVID-19*

Relaxation Practices (D)

Learning to relax is an essential component in moving past our trauma. It took years for us to become what abuse made us, and the path out is a lengthy one not quickly achieved.

Emotions and circumstances trigger the physical tension and stress These tensions have become stored in our bodies. These become manifested as outward behaviors and unmanageable symptoms. If we can find ways to relax the mind, our body will follow. When we can calm our nervous system through relaxation or meditation practices, we might be less likely to succumb to emotional instability.

When we relax using the following methods, we can train our minds and bodies to calm down; we will then think more transparently and handle our situations calmly. With practice, we can learn to do these methods rather quickly. When feeling anger or other volatile emotions rise, we can calm those emotions from erupting by pausing and taking time to breathe deeply in and out.

Although these exercises sound easy, it will take regular practice, repetition, commitment, and dedication to follow through with them. The results will be well worth the effort. Remember that results take time. Learning any new habits, we need to try and be patient with ourself. When we can get frustrated, annoyed and irritated easily, we need to affirm to ourself that anything new will take time.

Give yourself permission to be okay to feel whatever you feel.

Accept and allow emotions to surface and continue breathing. If you are new to these exercises, you will have scattered thoughts and uncomfortable emotions but let them come.

In practicing breathing exercises, there may be times it will be more effective when you are walking outside in nature or around where you live. It might also help if you play some calming instrumental music to help set the tone and atmosphere for relaxation. You can also light candles or infuse oils also to set the mood.

In fact, select one or two phrases from the following sentences and repeat them out loud or silently to yourself when you feel frustrated or impatient:

It is okay for me to be impatient.
It is okay for you to be frustrated.
It is okay for me to take longer, then I think I should.
It is okay to be right where I am at in this moment.
I have time, there is no hurry, there is nowhere to arrive.
In Christ, I can do this work.
Christ's love is in me all the time, even when I don't feel him.
I am never alone. Christ is always in me, even when I fear.

Breathing Practice (E)

In practicing breathwork, we want to be mindful of caring for ourselves in a kind and compassionate way. Practice the art of inviting fear, anger, rage as part of who you are and not pushing them away. Welcome them as friends and companions. Embrace them and draw them near and close. Acknowledge, accept, and permit them. Hold and cherish them. When we make friends with our darker emotions, we invite those parts of ourselves as intimate and necessary parts of who we are. We learn to integrate light and dark emotions when we are accepting of them.

Mindful breathing is an action that requires gentle caring for our own body, accepting and loving ourselves.

I will use the ocean waters to create a restful scene.

1. Begin to breathe deeply through your nose, hold the breath a few seconds and then exhale slowly out through the mouth.

    a. Breathe in deeply, evenly, and smoothly.

2. We can imagine lying on the water's surface, relaxing in its rhythmic waves of the in and out of the tide.

3. We can visualize some scenes or imagery while breathing deeply in, holding the breath, and then breathing slowly out through the mouth Imagine scenery that offers a sense of peace, joy, and safety.

4. Breath in, imagine being wrapped in warmth, safety, and light. Exhale, imagine the relief, letting go, and seeing stress or whatever is bothering you, leaving your body, joining the waters of the ocean. Imagine the waves as they rise and fall in rhythmic and melodic harmony.

5. Breathe in, opening your heart, and say, "Other people feel as I do too. This feeling I feel in my body is a feeling so many other persons felt from trauma. I am not a defect. I am not so abnormal as many feel just like me. It is normal to feel as I do from what happened to me. It is okay to feel. I can allow myself to feel."

6. What I am feeling is a normal reaction to what I have experienced. I can acknowledge, accept, and allow pain and suffering as part of my moving forward journey. I don't have to deny what I am feeling. I can share my feelings in the massive sea of suffering with others. Every human suffers.

7. I am breathing slowly, methodically, intentionally through my nose, holding the breath a few seconds, and then exhaling out my mouth. Breathe deeply in through the nose, hold the breath and slowly exhale, pushing out through the mouth.

    a. Frustrations will come. Yet we want to try not to focus on what is not happening. We want to be present in with the practice. Welcome the breathing cradle and embrace the breath as sacred. Exhale the air outwardly, pushing out the stress, the frustration, the irritation.

b. Exhale all that overwhelms (anxiety, depression, fear), and visualize each thing moving out through the mouth. Watch those energies moving into the open seas blending as one with the ocean waters. Imagine those energies leaving your mind and body, flowing out of you and pouring into the mass of waters.

c. Visualization is a powerful medium and has profound ramifications. What we think affects our mental, physical and spiritual being.

8. The practice involves scheduling time alone, repetition, regularity, and consistency. We want to engage in breathing exercises daily, regardless of the results.

The more we invest in breathwork, the more our bodies become acclimated. They will eventually respond in cooperating with the science behind the breathing. Over time, we will feel a bit more relaxed, less on edge, and more capable of regulating emotions, which in turn modifies behavior.

Progressive Relaxation Training (F)

This exercise aims to increase your muscles' tension. Hold it for five to ten seconds, and relax for ten to fifteen seconds. Be mindful and focus on one set of muscles at a time. Repeat each sequence as many times as necessary.

(Caution: *If you have an injury, physical pain, or are recovering from surgery, do not tense these areas.*)

1. Lie flat on your back or get into a comfortable seated position and close your eyes. Breathe deeply in through your nose, holding the breath, and then exhaling out through your mouth. Repeat this process slowly a few times to give your mind and body a chance to relax. Allow yourself to feel whatever you are feeling and sensing. It is okay to be anxious, frustrated, and overwhelmed in the beginning. Try not to focus on that, and just let your feelings exist.

2. Begin at the bottom part of your body, and stretch your legs out, pointing your toes away from your body, noting the tension in your ankles. Then turn your toes to your head, tensing your calves. Then let your feet fall to the floor, taking in a deep breath through your nose and letting go. Do this breathing in and out with the flexing of your legs a few times.

3. Working your way up the body, tighten your buttocks, then your thighs by pressing your heels as hard as you can into the floor and hold the breath in through your nose five to ten seconds, then let the breath go out through your open mouth. Breathe in slowly through your nose, keep it in for a few seconds, exhale out through your mouth, and relax.

4. Next, take in a deep breath filling your lungs, tighten your chest muscles, immediately tighten your stomach muscles, hold the air, and then exhale and relax.

5. Now arch your back slightly while keeping the rest of your body relaxed. You can notice the tension at your tailbone. Be aware of the stress in your spine and up to your neck. Hold this position as long as possible before slumping forward, exhaling as you relax your body and breath (do not do this if you have a back injury and avoid doing this if you have any pain).

6. The next step is to bend your elbows, tensing, and tightening your forearms, biceps while clenching your fists at the same time. Keep this tension and then straighten out your arms, shake out your hands. Take a deep breath in, hold for five to ten seconds, and then slowly let it out, relaxing your body.

7. Now hunch your shoulders, pull your head inward, pressing your chin to your chest, and tighten. Then drop your shoulders, allowing your head to fall forward, and slowly roll your head to the side and back of your neck. Reverse direction and move your head the other way. Take a deep breath in, hold it five to ten seconds, exhale out your mouth, allowing your neck, shoulders, and head to go limp.

8. Make a frown by wrinkling your forehead as tight as you can, then scrunch your eyes, flare your nostrils, and clench your jaw. Clench your lips and make an ugly face. Hold this position as tight as possible, breathing in, holding the breath, and then exhaling, letting go, and relaxing your facial muscles. Take another deep breath in, squinch your entire face, and then blow out, exhaling while relaxing all facial muscles.

9. Mentally visualize the entire procedure, and begin the exercise again, starting at your head, moving down to your face, chest, back, buttocks, thighs, legs, and feet. Breathe in deep and long through your nose, and then exhale out your mouth slowly, releasing any felt tension or stress as you move down your body, imagining the tension, worry, anxiety flowing down and out of your body as if in a liquid pool. Imagine it flowing out through your toes and into the expanse of the room.

10. If you notice any tension in a specific region of your body, focus on that part. Increase the tension. Tighten the entire section, and then take a deep breath, hold it a few seconds, exhaling, relaxing, and let go, blowing out all the stress.

11. As a licensed Tai Chi instructor, one of the cooldowns we end our practice with is standing and tensing our entire body. We tighten our whole body and take in a long slow deep breathe in through our nose and then hold the breath for several seconds. Then we exhale through our mouths, unclenching our bodies, slowly letting go and releasing any felt tension. The tension is tightened and then released three times. You could add this to the above technique as you end your progressive relaxation time.

While you are doing this relaxation training, visualize the stored stress energies moving through your body as a liquid and going out the top of your head and then moving out through your toes. As you progress up and down your body, scan for any tension and imagine it melting into this liquid pool, moving out away from your body.

Then imagine the liquid pool caressing your body, warming you on the inside and imagine this liquid is pure and holy. Imagine yourself lying in this pool, and it is holding you and carrying you. Imagine how peaceful this is and how still you feel.

Managing the breath is vital. Breathing slowly and deeply in, hold the breath five to ten seconds, and then slowly exhale into relaxation for ten to fifteen seconds before proceeding to the next sequence.

Visualization (G)

You can practice this next exercise anytime, even while doing chores. This practice is most beneficial to do after doing progressive relaxation exercise. Visualization is a valuable tool to use to combat stress, tension, and general unease. Once you gain the capacity to practice this exercise, you can then use it right in the moment of need to call up a peaceful, relaxing image or scene.

The concept is to think about and visualize in detail a time and place where you have felt safe, secure, and calm. When I started this practice, I imagined myself walking on a path through a forest with thick trees lining the right and the left sides of this path. I then imagined seeing the light at the end of this path as I continued walking.

When I arrived at the light, the scene opened up to a clearing where I saw a green meadow scattered with colorful wildflowers lying before me. The sun is always shining here, and its warmth soaks into the layers of my skin. I breathe in the smell of grass, flowers, and fresh air in this sanctuary in my mind. I then lie down in the middle of this lush, peaceful place and breathe in and out, relaxing and enjoying the solitude, the beauty, and the quiet. I imagine the sun warming, saturating, and filling me. I am in no hurry. I rest and relax in this place.

The other scene I call up is of the ocean. I imagine myself walking from the road to the beach, viewing the tall blades of grass as I walk on the path that opens to the expansive wide-open sea. I take off my shoes and step on the sand, feeling its warmth as I slowly walk closer to the water, hearing the rhythmic sound of the waves ebbing and flowing as the tide's rhythm lulls me inside, comforting.

I feel the warmth of the sand. I smell the salt air. I hear the gulls scream and see them flying on the air pockets as if not a worry in the world. I stand near the water's edge, allowing the waves' energizing power to lull me into a tranquil, peaceful state.

I view the horizon, sunshine with fluffy white clouds drifting. I stand with my eyes closed. My feet and legs are in the water and I hear the majestic crashing of the ocean waves hit against my body, and I feel its wetness. I am refreshed in this place.

You can create your own personal relaxation image and scene. You want to begin by closing your eyes and, as a painter, visualize the background coming to life in your mind. Fill in the details and add dimensions of time, place, shapes, colors, smells, sounds, light, and shadow.

Here are a few fragrances to use as prompts in creating your safe sanctuary; salt air, grass after it's mowed, a campfire burning, coffee brewing, candles burning, soup cooking, the rain, etc.

Be aware and sensitive to what you are seeing, hearing, sensing, touching. Notice the temperature, the warmth on your skin, the gentle breeze on your face, the feel of grass or sand on your feet, and remember the distinct smells and sounds. Hold the feelings of peace, tranquility, relaxation, and the reassuring sense of safety and security.

When you have created your scene, savor it, and cherish it as a sanctuary, you can go to again and again. Just like I did with my great-grandmother's farm. I repeatedly returned to capture the sense of peace, liberty, and safety known on those lands. Let all the sounds, sights, smells, images, and feelings to sink deeper into your psyche.

Name this scene—the farm, meadows, ocean—to attach these sensations and images to a word that your mind and body will connect to a state of peace and calm when you name this word again. You will remember the sense of peace, calm, and safety, and you can bring that into your present anytime you want.

Open your eyes and notice where you are in the world. Then close your eyes again and name the image you just created and allow yourself to become immersed in the entire scene. See it, hear it, feel it, touch it, taste it.

Notice the relaxing peace, calm, and safeness you sense in this place. Then open your eyes again and capture the sense of what you just felt and remember you can return to this place again and again and again. Just like I did with the "farm." You can add depth, character, and details or create a new scene.

You can use these techniques whenever you feel stressed, overwhelmed, or tense. Or you can use them to begin or end your day as a meditation. Practicing visualization a bit each day will gradually decrease your feelings of stress while also reducing inordinate expressions of anger and rage.

When you create your scene, imagine all that you are feeling, tasting, touching, smelling, and hearing, including all the senses in your sanctuary.

Here is a list to help prompt you in creating your special sanctuaries:

Location: Forest, waterfall, lake, creek, ocean, mountain, valley, field.
Time: Morning, noon, midday, night.
Emotions: Happy, peaceful, quiet, still, safety, calm.
Sensations: Texture/touch/feel (soft, hard, liquid, warmth, cold)
Imagery: What do you see? Clouds, flowers, sun, moon, stars, fire-
    flies, campfire, rainbow.

Imagery (H)

Imagery and visualization are similar techniques used to help in managing symptoms and promoting well-being. The following exercise enables you to imagine your thoughts as if floating down a stream or river.

1. Get into a comfortable position. Sit in a chair. Lie on your back. Just be at ease in whatever place you want to be. Notice your body and breath. Be aware of the sense of your

body resting, not having to do anything. Breathe deeply in and out for a few moments, sensing your rhythm.

2. Now imagine a river or brook that is continuously flowing and moving. Picture what surrounds it, grass, plants, trees, flowers, rocks, etc. Visualize the bright sunshine of a fall day where the sky is bluest of blues, and a few white clouds scatter the horizon. Hear the gentle breeze blowing and feel it softly brush your face. Picture the trees clothed in glorious colors and various shades of rust, burnt-orange, yellow and red. Smell the air as if you are sitting on the bank of the water's edge, surrounded by the solitude of nature. Capture the sense of peace, safety, and stillness in this place. You are alone, and the only sounds you hear are birds, the soft gurgling of the water, and the wind rustling leaves. There is nothing you have to do. There is nowhere you have to be. You have all the time in the world. There is no hurry. There is no rush.

3. Now imagine the leaves of the trees have fallen onto the water's surface and are carried downstream. Take whatever you are thinking, one thought at a time, and place it on one of these leaves and watch it being carried away from you downstream. Imagine putting the idea of what worries you on one of the leaves. Watch as it is moving slowly away from your mind and your view. It is gradually being carried downstream, further away from you, relieving you of that sense.

4. Visualize each thought that bothers you and place it on one of the colored leaves on the water's surface. See it, watch it, and notice it moves further away from you and carried down the river where it will gather with the other thought leaves in a collected pool of your most unmanageable symptoms.

5. Now do this with what you fear, what is causing anxiety? And what depresses?

6. The thoughts you are placing on these leaves are, *I fear I cannot change. I worry I will be like this forever. I am sick of feeling depressed. I will never get well.*

7. Sit with this picture and soak in all you see, hear, taste, touch, and smell in this place. Continue breathing slowing and deeply in and out as you place each thought, each word, each sentence on a leaf. Watch it being carried away from your thoughts, your body, and your heart. Also, place any other idea, even the good ones, on a leaf and do this same exercise in your mind, watching it slowly drift downstream, away from you.

8. Imagine this river or water is the Holy Spirit carrying these thoughts and these emotions into the spiritual realm and near God's heart. Imagine each thought is collected in a place where they will no longer have control over you. Imagine how free you will feel and be when no longer ruled by these thoughts or emotions. Visualize your freedom in this place and imagine yourself now in a glass-bottom boat drifting down this same waterway or river.

9. You are in this boat, and all you have to do is relax, rest, and let this boat carry you down this waterway. You do not have to put in the effort to row or move the boat. All you have to do is sit or lie in it and perhaps view the clouds and sky above as you rest. You have nowhere to be and nowhere to go and nothing to achieve. You can allow this boat to do all it needs to do to take you to this place of rested peace and inner joy of God and his love for you.

10. Imagine your life as if in a boat, and the water is the heart of God holding, carrying, and caring for you. He is the provider and the doer. He is the performer working in you the gifts of holiness, righteousness, and love.

11. Visualize this scene when you are overwhelmed, frightened, anxious, or depressed. Picture God as the expansive and endless realm of love as the glistening sun upon the water. Imagine the sun, the glorious colors, and the fragrant smell of fall as traits of his character and love for you. He wants

to create beauty and wonder in you. You are made from beauty and wonder and you are returning home to this beauty and wonder.

12. Now picture the beauty in this scene as God's beauty within you.

13. Imagine God is surrounding, filling, and saturating you with kindness, goodness, gentleness, compassion.

14. His love is embracing, holding, and carrying you right where you are, as you are, right now, this moment into his sacred dwelling and heart within you. His love envelopes, fills and encases you, protecting.

15. Receive this filling, and all God desires to pour into you from his fullness and his bounty. Take as long as you need to remind yourself you are the goodness of God, and you are the human vessel that carries all he is, right where you are, just as you are, and in this season and at this time. You are loved. You are love.

The Dan Tian Breathing Method in Breathing (I)

This breathing method is created based on traditional qigong and modern medical research into the deep stabilizer muscles. It is useful to facilitate sinking qi to the dan tian and to enhance qi power, in turn improving internal energy.

You can practice breathing, either sitting or standing upright. Be aware of holding the correct posture.

10. Put left hand on your abdomen just above the belly button and right hand below it. Concentrate on your lower abdomen and the pelvic floor muscle.

11. When you inhale, expand your lower abdominal area—allow it to bulge out a little—and let your abdominal and pelvic floor muscles relax. You should feel a slight push out of the right hand.

12. As you exhale, gently contract the pelvic floor muscles and the lower abdomen. Feel the contraction of the power with

your right hand, keeping the area above your belly button as still as possible. Contract the pelvic floor muscles very gently, so gently that it's almost like you're just thinking about contracting them.

13. Another good way is to imagine that you're bringing your pelvic floor just half an inch closer to your belly button. A more forceful contraction would move the left hand too much, and that would mean involving different groups of muscles, therefore not be as effective.

14. As you inhale and relax the pelvic and lower abdominal muscles, try not to loosen them completely but retain approximately 10–20 percent of the contraction. Breathing in, holding the breath, then breathing out exhaling will allow you to maintain an upright posture and have the right group of muscles ready for the next phase.

Practice it regularly, and you will find it easier to do; as you practice your tai chi forms, apply this method as often as comfortable to you. There is no need to be conscious of this breathing 100% of the time. Whenever you feel uncomfortable, simply let go and breathe naturally.

If you can feel the qi, gently push it down along the conception vessel on expiration and up along the governing vessel. Another right way is to visualize your qi move in a straight line just beneath your skin: up to the middle of your sternum (the point below two nipples) on inspiration and down to the dan tian on expiration.[1]

Gratitude Practice (J)

The most popular gratitude exercise is Martin Seligman's Three Good Things (e.g., https://happyproject.in/three-good-things/). It may be difficult to find three good things each day when you find

---

[1.] This Dan Tien breathing method article is from Dr. Paul Lam's Tai Chi for Health Institute's webpage under the article section titled: Tai Chi Breathing. (https://taichiforhealthinstitute.org/articles/tai-chi/)

yourself in a "hellhole," but it always possible to discover three hidden blessings in all the problems you have to endure.

Try the following existential gratitude exercises:

- Discover three opportunities in today's troubled world.
- Express thanks to someone who still cares for you in difficult times.
- Feel grateful that you still have the gift of life because there is always hope as long as you can breathe.
- Give thanks that this disaster brings out the generosity and altruism in so many people.
- Feel grateful for all the frontline healthcare workers who risk their own lives to care for others.
- Feel thankful for our government, who can take care of their citizens and rally all the resources in the mortal combat against the pandemic.

I bet you will feel much better after doing the above exercise for just 3 minutes a day. That is the magic power of gratitude.

—According to Viktor E. Frankl and Paul T. P. Wong, *Made for Resilience and Happiness: Effective Coping with COVID-19*

Try the following exercise taken from Paul Wong's blog website:

Try this life-changing gratitude exercise. It is one of the many existential positive interventions in meaning therapy:

- Be thankful for your life with all its creative contributions.
- Be thankful for your family and friends and all those who have contributed to your life.
- Be thankful for nature or the Creator for giving us the beautiful planet earth as our home.

If you meditate on the three areas daily, it
will make you a better and happier person.

—Paulwong.wordpress.com

Here are some other considerations to retrain one's mind toward
an attitude of gratitude.

- Focus on what is true and good. Reviewing what you
  appreciate and are thankful for will help retrain your mind
  to naturally and regularly see the good rather than obsessing on negatives.
- Redirect negative thinking. Instead of saying to yourself, "I
  will never reach my goal," redirect this thought by reflecting on how far you have come, what you are capable of,
  and what you have in your life right now that matters.
- Do something nice for someone, even a stranger. When
  we start thinking of how we can help others, it retrains our
  brains to focus less on what is "wrong" with us, and we
  begin to think how we can be of help to others.
- Say what you appreciate in the other. When with another,
  try to recognize a trait in them that you admire and let
  them know about it. This also retrains us from over focusing on what you don't like about another and retraining
  our minds to appreciate the good, kind, and compassionate
  traits in someone.
- Keep a gratitude journal. Each day, take a few moments
  and write each thing you appreciate and are thankful for,
  no matter how small. Review these items each morning
  upon awakening, and then again in the evening before
  retiring.
- Listen. Listen to the birds, the wind, the music, and the
  sounds around you in stillness and quiet. Listen carefully
  when someone is speaking. Learning to listen and not react
  or talk helps train us toward sensitivity and discernment.
  Listen to God's voice among the chatter—knowing his

voice always leads in peace, care, compassion, mercy, and love.

- Smile. Practice smiling throughout the day. Even when you don't feel like it, smile. Smile at others you live with. Smile at yourself. Smile when discouraged or fearful. This is also an exercise that trains your mind that smiling is okay, even when you don't feel okay.

Trying to see the good in your daily life or relationships and expressing this, means you are putting forward an energy of gratitude and appreciation. This is not denying reality or emotions, it practices that smiling is teaching and retraining our minds to be thankful in ways, perhaps, we were never taught. This may feel foreign to you at first but continue to apply these small changes in what you think on, and over time, you will recognize a shift in your attitude where these affirming types of thoughts and responses will become more natural and more obvious to you.

Mindfulness practice retrains our minds with an emphasis on what we appreciate, the goodness we see, and the things we are thankful for, building new neuropathways. With regularity, consistency, and daily practice, over time, our minds will think more towards the good, the light, and the truer gifts in life. We will become less introspective on what is "wrong" with us, and we will begin to be "other-centered."

Grieving Losses (K)

Having suffered trauma, I recognized my need to grieve the losses. I had to accept and let go of these losses, regrets, sorrows in my own healing journey.

The loss of what I could have accomplished. The loss of who I could have been earlier in my life. The loss of childhood. The loss of a nurturing dad. The loss of integration as a person. The loss of belonging, connectedness, and bonding to myself, God, and others as a young adult. The loss of many years of struggling and suffering in not understanding how to find my way out of living hell.

Losses are painful, but there are methods we can use that broadens our ability to cope and ones that build resilience in the face of suffering. Grieving losses become the critical path in and through recovering from the effects of abuse. I suggest you utilize the chapter on "Necessary Processes" and use the acknowledging, accepting, and allowing to mourn each loss you experienced.

Grieving, mourning, and accepting these losses will be vital so that the losses do not remain stuck and hinder the forward moving process.

Resources for Additional Help

Dr. Paul Wong—International Network on Personal Meaning: https://www.meaning.ca/
National Council for Behavioral Health: https://www.thenationalcouncil.org/areas-of-expertise/trauma-informed-behavioral-healthcare/

The following two links will take you to the Positive Psychology website full of resources:
https://positivepsychology.com/
https://positivepsychology.com/emotion-regulation-worksheets-strategies-dbt-skills/

Benefit and uses of EFT Tapping:
https://www.verywellhealth.com/the-benefits-of-tapping-90029#:~:text=In%20alternative%20medicin

Focus on the Family Website:
https://www.focusonthefamily.com/family-qa/mindfulness-a-christian-approach/

Phases of Trauma Healing: Part I, Establishing Safety:
https://www.goodtherapy.org/blog/phases-of-trauma-healing-part-i-establishing-safety/

Apollo becomes another toolbox tool to help you when you need it by helping to retrain our nervous systems to be more balanced and resilient in the face of stress over time:
https://apolloneuro.com/how-it-works/

How Dance Therapy Helps Heal Trauma:
https://www.dancemagazine.com/dance-as-a-healing-art-2647439136.html
https://oritkrug.com/how-dance-movement-therapy-heals-trauma/
https://dancingwithclass.org/trauma-informed-dance/

We are a transformative education company partnering with the world's top teachers, experts, and healers to support your personal learning journey:
https://theshiftnetwork.com/?&utm_medium=affiliate&utm_source=infusionsoft&cookieUUID=a9d4e266-f246-4993-9e05-ff-c7a1e7f092

Trauma-Informed Expressive Arts Therapy:
https://www.psychologytoday.com/us/blog/arts-and-health/201203/trauma-informed-expressive-arts-therapy

Top Ten Art Therapy Visual Journaling Prompts:
https://www.psychologytoday.com/us/blog/arts-and-health/201311/top-ten-art-therapy-visual-journaling-prompts

ABOUT THE AUTHOR

Lorraine Taylor is a passionate non-credentialed teaching lay minister and an enthusiastic speaker at events, groups, and churches. She is an engaged leader and facilitates teaching a weekly online community of faith that embraces interdenominational and non-affiliated members.

Over the span of thirty-five years, Lorraine has passionately served in mentoring, modeling, and instructing in the way of Christ. Her warm personality and Gospel message of grace captivates hearts young and old. Her extensive background includes leadership training and program development with individuals and groups in the corporate, political, and ministry realms. As a former therapist, she specialized in individual and group counseling in the fields of post-addiction treatment, adult disabilities and individuals who experienced trauma. Lorraine's long-time endeavor has been serving her region as a volunteer community advocate experienced in: spiritual abuse, trauma, partner violence, family systems, disenfranchised populations, human service agencies, housing, disability, and medical issues. Early in her career, she published weekly as a photojournalist. Lorraine has also published numerous devotionals and biblical articles in the US as well as internationally.

If you were to stop by Lorraine's home, she would invite you in for a cup of organically brewed herbal tea and a taste of one of her delicious homemade culinary treats. She is a promoter of health and wellness, reads and researches diverse material, is an enthusiastic nature photography, avidly gardens edibles, plants and flowers, is a fermenter of foods and beverages, and gains much pleasure walking and hiking trails. She is community centered, thrives on interconnecting with new people, engaging in meaningful relationships, lively conversations and is a life-long learner. She resides in Upstate New York with her husband.

Credentials

Masters-level degree in rehabilitation counseling from Syracuse University (*Summa cum Laude*), Syracuse, New York.

International Tai Chi Instructor and board-certified with The Tai Chi for Health Institute in Sydney, Australia.
https://taichiforhealthinstitute.org/

Certified facilitator for One Circle Foundation young girls programming
https://onecirclefoundation.org/

Memberships:
NAMI (National Alliance of Mental Illness)
https://www.nami.org/Home

INPM (International Network on Personal Meaning)
http://www.inpm.org/

https://www.faithwriters.com/websites/my_website.php?id=71379

Contact the author for speaking/teaching events/groups/conferences at livingintentionally75@gmail.com